POEMS FROM AFRICA

POEMS
FROM
AFRICA

Selected by Samuel Allen

Drawings by Romare Bearden

Thomas Y. Crowell Company

New York

DESIGNED BY MARSHA COHEN AND MINA BAYLIS

Manufactured in the United States of America

Copyright acknowledgments will be found beginning on page 191.

Library of Congress Cataloging in Publication Data
Allen, Samuel   comp.   Poems from Africa.
(Poems of the world)   1.   African poetry.   I.   Title.
PL8013.E5A4   1973   808.81'00967   75–184978
ISBN 0–690–62975–3

1   2   3   4   5   6   7   8   9   10

896
Dee. 3 73

To Alioune Diop and Richard Wright
who labored together in the cause of Africa
and to Marie-Christine

Poems of the World

Under the editorship of Lillian Morrison

POEMS FROM AFRICA
   Selected by Samuel Allen

POEMS FROM FRANCE
   Selected by William Jay Smith

POEMS FROM THE GERMAN
   Selected by Helen Plotz

POEMS FROM THE HEBREW
   Selected by Robert Mezey

POEMS FROM INDIA
   Selected by Daisy Aldan

POEMS FROM IRELAND
   Selected by William Cole

POEMS FROM ITALY
   Selected by William Jay Smith

In Preparation:

POEMS FROM LATIN AMERICA
   Selected by Norman Thomas di Giovanni

Editor's Acknowledgments

The editor is keenly aware that, for a variety of reasons, anthologies never, finally, succeed in including every author of merit. This we can only regret. We should point out, however, that for practical reasons we have limited ourselves to poems composed originally either in English or in French, except, of course, for the oral tradition.

I wish to acknowledge the opportunity afforded by Tuskegee Institute and Wesleyan University to complete this volume. Without the time made available, largely through the interest and cooperation of Dr. Youra Qualls and Dr. William Coley of those institutions, the work would not have been accomplished within any foreseeable period.

Obtaining permissions from wandering poets in several different countries across the sea could be an impossible goal. Miss Susan Caughman at Boston University worked efficiently and tirelessly to make it possible. She aided greatly in the preparation of the final manuscript and also managed, remarkably, to cast a ray of light into the thicket of the copyright law. Mr. Ezekiel Mphahlele, the noted South African novelist and critic, was fortunately in the country teaching at Denver University, and was kind enough to offer suggestions which proved invaluable in locating those poets we had been unable to reach.

Especially helpful was the editorial advice of Miss Lynette Innes at Cornell University, whose knowledge of African literature and keen critical judgment were of great assistance in shaping this material.

It is our rare fortune that this volume is illustrated by Romare Bearden. His famed talent has probed deeply, over the years, the consciousness of the African of the diaspora.

I wish, finally, to express my thanks to the poets of the homeland, through whose vision the ancestors and the yet unborn may ultimately be rejoined.

SAMUEL ALLEN

Contents

Introduction   *1*

Prologue   *15*

ORAL TRADITION   *19*

WEST AFRICA (in English)   *57*

WEST AFRICA (translated from the French)   *97*

SOUTH AFRICA   *127*

EAST AFRICA   *141*

Epilogue   *175*

Biographies of the Poets   *181*

Copyright Acknowledgments   *191*

Index of Titles   *195*

Index of Poets   *199*

Index of Translators   *201*

Index of First Lines   *203*

Introduction

To enter into another culture is to risk misunderstanding. The danger is lessened, however, if we are introduced through the creative arts. As we approach another community of men, we become aware that poetry is one of the best roads to understanding. The poems in this book are of interest not only for their beauty, but also for the insights they afford into societies of great cultural wealth whose image has for so long been dominated by the popular distortions of an Edgar Rice Burroughs, a Vachel Lindsay, or a mindless cartoon television industry.

The poems are not presented in precise historical sequence, but the oral tradition with which the collection starts was indeed the beginning, a beginning which fortunately still survives. Oral poetry is one of the strongest elements in the African cultural pattern; its riches are evident in the deep and often oracular sense of wisdom and in the imaginative flair of these representative pieces. Inevitably there is a twofold loss: first, in reducing the living word, whether spoken or sung, to the printed page; and secondly, in translating it from the language in which it first was uttered. There is nothing to be done about that, unhappily; the majority of us will never know the original African languages. There is still, however, a veritable treasure which comes through, yielding a glimpse of a rich poetic tradition which has prevailed for centuries across the African continent.

The range of subjects is vast as the poet at evening in the village circle explores the concerns of man. His vision is not an idealized one; it can be and usually is very earthy and matter-of-fact, even when dealing with the activities of the gods. This earthy quality gives pith and reality to the poems. They can move from a prosaic hunger for food to a warrior's starkly magnificent embrace of destiny:

I am sharpening my sword:
O High God, if you wish
You may give me
What you wish.
What will fall in front of me
Is what you give me.
What you do not give me
I cannot find.

The African's creative encounter with divinity has yielded a vivid imagery. The great god Obatala has many powers; it is he who "turns blood into children." We are, indeed, all children in God's eyes. Who can know the ways of Shango! The divinity is beyond knowing; he is "the depth too deep for the measure stick!"

We find here views of life and of the cosmos evolved over the centuries, as men grappled with the powerful and mysterious forces of their environment and sought to find meaning in the chaos. Sometimes we hear simply a lament over an unhappy fate; sometimes we sense a will to impose order and purpose upon events. There is compassion for the sick orphan who "is dying to see its mother." We grieve with the blind boy as the train indifferently carries others to their destination and "the blind boy to his distress." There is the eloquent and simple lament which has an oddly current ring:

"Oh, Ozidi my man, my man, my man,
        my man!
Oh leader of the vanguard, my man,
        my man, my man!"

Death is for the African, as it is for all, implacable; but we find here, also, a deep sense of assurance. All men wait for death:

for him who will come and will say:
"Come" to the one and "Go" to the other.

> He will say "Come" to the one and
> "Go" to the other
> and God will be with his children.
> and God will be with his children.

There is an expression of the sterner side of life, but there is also a rich sense of humor in this poetry. Here, for example, is an unusual but enterprising advocate of the law:

> Come here, my beloved,
> Come, give me a kiss.
> There is a new law
> Which says we must embrace each other.

At least there is one among the Zulu concerned with law and order. He hopes to make it two. The Ziba maiden has no desire at all to get married:

> But father and mother compel me to,
> And so I am willing to give it a try.

The "Trouble-Lover" meets his match when he marries the "wife" of Shango (the God of thunder):

> belching fire from her mouth
> whene'er she spoke.

The lady declares her deathless loyalty to her husband, but it seems she is a practical lady:

> O my husband, when you die I will die with you.
> .   .   .   .
> No sooner is the husband dead than this Tough Lady goes
> over to another man.

A father in this country would be no doubt startled, but delighted to receive tribute such as this:

> Hail him
> One who says and does it.
> It is father.

In contrast to the fierce reaction to European colonization expressed by some of the modern poets, the oral tradition views the intruder critically but with some amusement:

> A baby is a European
> *he does not eat our food:*
> he drinks from his own waterpot.
>
> .   :   .   .
>
> A baby is a European
> *he cares very little for others;*
> he forces his will upon his parents.

Although there is an awareness of grief as an inevitable part of man's lot, this oral tradition reflects a vigorous and purposeful life with a full measure of satisfaction, as well as sorrow, within a framework of meaning and fulfillment. With the coming of the European and modernization, we see developing an anguish within the outlook of the African. The poet gazes about him to discover that his old culture is shattered and that he and his people live in a world shaped by forces of which they are not a part.

It is with the twentieth-century poet of the written word that we watch the troubled meeting of the ancient lore with the modern African sensibility, now exploring subjects beyond the boundaries of its former concern. These poets express vividly the situation of the African today, coming to grips with the Western world, searching out the unmapped area between the old ways and the new.

Beginning in the late thirties, the work of a group of African and Afro-Caribbean poets formed itself into a trend which came

to be known as negritude. Outstanding among those from the Western Hemisphere were Aimé Césaire of Martinique and Léon Damas
of French Guyana. Those from West Africa included Léopold
Sédar Senghor, David Diop, and Birago Diop of Senegal. Their
work attacked the evils of French colonialism, repudiated France
as a cultural model, and asserted a distinctively African heritage.
Most productive in the nineteen forties and fifties, negritude was a
revindication of the self-esteem of the African, a rejection of European cultural domination in favor of an authentic African identity.
In a famous poem, "Black Woman," Senghor extols her beauty:

> Naked woman, dark woman
> Firm-fleshed ripe fruit, sombre raptures
>   of black wine, mouth making lyrical my mouth . . . .
> Your solemn contralto voice is the spiritual
>   song of the Beloved.

The same subject is the theme of David Diop's "Rama Kam," which
is unexcelled as an example of another important aspect of negritude—the powerful and frequently intricate rhythmic pattern in the
poetry.

It has been pointed out that rhythm in poetry, in song, and in
dance (frequently one unified pattern in the African tradition) is
at the heart of the religious experience in some African societies.
There is, according to this view, a vital force which is the key ele-
ment in all creation, a kind of life force or energy both physical and
spiritual in nature. All things are animated by this vital force. And
it is the rhythmic pattern which invokes it. The world view assumed
in Africa by this way of thinking is commonly known as "animism."
(The religious aspect has been of special interest here in the United
States, where rhythmic skill was at one time considered an ele-
mentary and unimportant talent of the Afro-American musicians
who created jazz.)

One of the best known poems reflecting this animist view is

Birago Diop's "Souffles" (in English, "Breaths"), in which he vividly, with a flawless craft, expresses the communion of the living and the dead, the departed but present ancestors:

> Listen more often to things than to beings
> Hear the fire's voice,
> Hear the voice of water.
> Hear, in the wind, the sobbing of the trees.
> It is the breath of the ancestors.

The Africans writing in English were later in developing a substantial body of accomplished poetry; it was in the late fifties and the sixties that the work of Wole Soyinka, J. P. Clark, Gabriel Okara, Christopher Okigbo, and others appeared. Instead of following in the path of the French-speaking African poets, they ignored or rejected negritude. The poetry of negritude had focused chiefly upon matters of public interest; it was an attack upon European racism and its cultural and political domination, a rediscovery of Africa's past glory. The Nigerian poets, particularly, turned from these public themes to individual concerns. To the extent that their work did assume a public stance, it had more to do with Africa internally than with a rejection of Europe.

There is a variety of eloquent voices in this poetry. Christopher Okigbo, for some the most significant African poet writing in the English language, is not easily understood (which seems to be a way with "significant" poets). Yet, in spite of the sometimes difficult language, the poetry communicates. His is a spiritual quest in which we see both Christian and animist imagery. His compatriot, Soyinka, has said that Okigbo succeeds in the African poet's mission to achieve in his work the coming together of the material and the spiritual levels. Okigbo was an Ibo (the people who, basically, constituted the Biafran Republic) and a man prepared to live his convictions. He gave his own answer to the question of the relationship of art to politics, risking his life from the earliest days in support of the abortive Biafran state. Finally, while still a young man, he died a soldier in the Biafran army.

The poetry of Soyinka and Clark grows out of the same African tradition, perceiving a life force in nature as well as in man. In "Season" Soyinka finds a living pulse within the slow process of rust:

> Rust is ripeness, rust
> And the wilted corn-plume.
>
> .   .   .   .
>
> Laden stalks
> Ride the germ's decay—we await
> The promise of the rust.

We feel the deep mystic strain of J. P. Clark as he recalls how, as a boy, he woke late one night to hear the rain falling and his mother moving about to secure the house.

> What time of night it is
> I do not know
> Except that like some fish
> Doped out of the deep
> I have bobbed up bellywise
> From stream of sleep
> And no cocks crow.
> It is drumming hard here
> And I suppose everywhere
> Droning with insistent ardour upon
> Our roof thatch and shed
>
> .   .   .   .
>
> We have drunk tonight of a spell
> Deeper than the owl's or bat's
> That wet of wings may not fly.

Returning for a moment to Senegal, we remember how the same deep spell of the African night enveloped Senghor:

> Toko'Waly my uncle, do you remember those
>   distant nights when my head grew heavy
>   against the patience of your back?
> Or holding me by the hand, your hand led me
>   through the shadows and signs?
> The fields are flowers of glow worms; the stars
>   come to rest on the grass, on the trees.
> All around is silence.
> Only the droning scents of the bush, hives of
>   red bees drowning the stridulation of the crickets
> And the muffled tom-tom, the far-off breathing
>   of the night.

In East Africa, too, nature holds a certain mystery and a sense of life constantly renewed. In "Kariuki," by the Kenyan poet Joseph Gatuiria, an old man with the ancient wisdom of his people enters the house of the newborn baby:

> "How are you, Kariuki?" This he whispers
> To the deaf stranger of this world.
>
>   .   .   .   .
>
> "It's a boy?" "Kariuki is born!"
> The old warrior is born again.

In the West African poetry, the turning away from public issues is nowhere more aptly stated than in "Voices" by Ken Tsaro-Wiwa:

> They speak of taxes
> Of oil and power
>
> They speak of honour
> And pride of tribe

They speak of war
Of bows and arrows

They speak of tanks
And putrid human flesh

I sing my love
For Maria.

In "The Pigeon-Hole" Mabel Segun paints a poignant picture of a young girl confused not by affairs of state, but by the tormenting problem of growing up:

If only I knew for certain
What my delinquent self would do . . .
But I never know
until the deed is done
and I live on fearing,
wondering which part of me will be supreme—
the old and tested one, the present
or the future unknown.
Sometimes all three have equal power
and then
how I long for a pigeon-hole.

While these poets were not absorbed to the same degree in the earlier challenge to Europe, their work does reflect the culture clash, as the ancestors, for example, confront O'Hare Airport. As Okogbule Wonodi's plane approaches, he sees beyond the darkness

. . . ten dainty maidens
And beside them ten young men in loincloths
And he brought the sacred drums and drumsticks
And walked before them; and the maidens
And the young men gave their waists to the drum

And his voice dug deep into the Fathers.
They danced behind him, frenzied as prophets.
Sweating, beating a staccato of sounds,
He was one with them, lost to the moment.

"This is O'Hare"
                    and the dancers sank
fast over fast-running pillars of light.

Other poets react, each in his own way, to the coming of a new
society. Aig Higo, perhaps not altogether humorously, warns:

My background is working class
My foreground is working class
I am myself my slogan
Eat, booze and be married
For tomorrow we vote.

Joe de Graft, a visitor to the "New World," sees man diminished
by the soaring technological triumphs of a New York City: "Man,
The city builder/ Man, The world girdler/ Man, The rejected
prayer."

The twentieth century is witnessing a renewal of the arts throughout Africa, but for a long period, while this was evident in the
western and the southern parts of the continent, in the East there
was silence. With the poets from Kenya, Uganda, and other eastern
areas represented in this collection, this situation is beginning to
change, and we see East Africa moving to join the rest of the
continent. David Rubadiri describes the fateful moment when the
black king says, "White man you are welcome," and "the west is let
in." In the remarkable long poem "Song of Lawino," by Okot
p'Bitek, we have a dramatic and compelling account of the con-
frontation of old Africa with the new ways of Europe. It has proved
to be a controversial work in the poet's homeland (Uganda). The

narrator of the poem, an Acoli housewife, is less than enthusiastic, for example, about the schools of the new order:

> You think of the pleasures
> Of the girls
> Dancing before their lovers,
>
> Then you look at the teacher
> Barking meaninglessly
> Like the yellow monkey.

Later, she is ironic in her description of the manners of her "educated" husband:

> And when visitors have arrived
> My husband's face darkens,
> He never asks you in,
> And for greeting
> He says
> "What can I do for you?"

Obviously, in societies moving more and more toward modernity, willingly or no, such a critical mood would strike a jarring note. The poem, however, possesses an exceptional dramatic force and is eloquent in its affirmation of the old traditions.

In the modern poetry of South Africa, there is one major theme —the continued suffering of an oppressed people. The expression of pain and outrage in this poetry is similar to that of the earlier poetry of negritude in the period before African nations began to gain freedom. We hear the ominous sound of the police boot on the door and the cries of torture under apartheid (that system in South Africa under which the Africans are rigidly excluded from the areas occupied by whites, except for work, and by which white domination is maintained):

The sounds begin again;
the siren in the night
the thunder at the door
the shriek of nerves in pain.

Then the keening crescendo
of faces split by pain
the wordless, endless wail
only the unfree know.

A Zulu "lyric" describes the infamous pass system in South Africa and, briefly, with stark eloquence, makes real the tragedy which has befallen the country:

Take off your hat.
What is your home name?
Who is your father?
Who is your chief?
Where do you pay your tax?
What river do you drink?
We mourn for our country.

The earlier poets of the modern era expressed a deep nostalgia for an ancestral way of life, and tended to glorify it much as the poets of the Renaissance glorified European antiquity. Some of the newer poetry is moving now to appraise and to criticize African societies, and to look toward change. Kwesi Brew, a diplomat in Ghana's foreign service, laments the dead hand of the past. In "Ancestral Faces" the spirits returned from generations past and

Saw the same men, slightly wizened,
Shuffle their sandalled feet to the same rhythms.
They heard the same words of wisdom uttered
Between puffs of pale blue smoke.
They saw us,
And said! They have not changed!

In similar vein, the brilliant and caustic Soyinka has written a long creation myth, *Idandre,* in which he extols those Yorbua gods who open the way toward change.

> The world was choked in wet embrace
> Of serpent spawn, waiting Ajantala's rebel birth
> Monster child, wrestling pachyderms of myth,
>
> .   .   .   .
>
> may we celebrate the stray electron, defiant
> Of patterns, celebrate the splitting of the gods
> Canonization of the strong hand of a slave who set
> The rock in revolution—
> All hail Saint Atunda, First revolutionary
> Grand iconoclast at genesis.

Finally, the poems are here to speak for themselves, alive and meaningful beyond any opinion we may have to offer. Africa is no longer the "dark continent" in the old unhappy sense, and indeed, it never was. Yet it is difficult in these lines not to feel the mystery which the poets feel, profoundly real in the huge African night to which they bring a witness; not to sense with them in the silence "the depth too deep for the measure stick." Perhaps, in the immensity of that night not yet outraged by neon, the ancestors pause to listen as a continent stirs and Africa moves toward a renewed encounter with her destiny.

PROLOGUE

CHRISTINA AMA ATA AIDOO

(Ghana)

from *Sebonwoma*

I would like to go
    Where
In days of old
    The Aged
    Sharp-eyed
    Hardknuckled
    Sages of our race
Kept in silent grove and dark,
    The sacred Lore.

ORAL TRADITION

Invocation of the Creator

He is patient, he is not angry.
He sits in silence to pass judgement.
He sees you even when he is not looking.
He stays in a far place—but his eyes are on the town.

He stands by his children and lets them succeed.
He causes them to laugh—and they laugh.
Ohoho—the father of laughter.
His eye is full of joy.
He rests in the sky like a swarm of bees.

Obatala—who turns blood into children.

Translator: Ulli Beier

Song for the Sun that Disappeared Behind the Rainclouds

The fire darkens, the wood turns black.
The flame extinguishes, misfortune upon us.
God sets out in search of the sun.
The rainbow sparkles in his hand,
the bow of the divine hunter.
He has heard the lamentations of his children.

He walks along the milky way, he collects the stars.
With quick arms he piles them into a basket
piles them up with quick arms
like a woman who collects lizards
and piles them into her pot, piles them up
until the pot overflows with lizards
until the basket overflows with light.

Translator: P. Trilles

YORUBA

Shango, I Prostrate to You Every Morning

Shango, I prostrate to you every morning,
Before I set out to do anything.

The dog stays in the house of its master
But it does not know his intentions.
The sheep does not know the intentions
Of the man who feeds it.
We ourselves follow Shango
Although we do not know his intentions.
It is not easy to live in Shango's company.

When the crab leaves its hole,
We do not know which direction it is taking.
Shango went to Ibadan and arrived at Ilorin.

Translators: Bakare Gbadamosi
Ulli Beier

from *Song of Praise to the Creator*

Invocation

Perfection ever rising to perfection,
The man who fashioned mountains and rocks!
Purity Immaculate,
Wood white and unblemished.

Guardian of nation upon nation,
Lone creator of firmament and horizon!
Origin of nation upon nation!
Even before birth the King!

The one of there! The one of here!
The one of here! The one of there!
The one everywhere, above and below!
The knower of all!
The beautiful, knower of the innermost!
Lord of wisdom, above and below!
The depth too deep for the measure stick.

Lord of heaven's vault!
Lord of that which endeth not! Lord of the everlasting!
The rock which has withstood the fire!
Lord of that which endeth not, both the going out and
    the coming back.

Translator: G. H. Franz

Love Songs

1.

I sleep long and soundly,
Suddenly the door creaks,
Confused, I open my eyes,
And find my love standing there:
What matters death to me?

2.

It has been raining and raining,
It has been raining and raining,
I go out to leave my footprints:
I see the footprints of my love.

3.

He has two loves,
He has two loves,
I go to see him off.
I meet the other woman.
I cannot go on,
I cannot go back,
I burst into tears.
Translator: J. H. Kwabena Nketia

Household Song

When I asked for him at Entoto, he was towards Akaki,
So they told me;
When I asked for him at Akaki, he was towards Jarer,
So they told me;
When I asked for him at Jarer, he was at Mendar,
So they told me;
When I asked for him at Mendar, he was towards Awash,
So they told me;
When I asked for him at Awash, he was towards Chercher,
So they told me;
When I asked for him at Chercher, he was towards Harar,
So they told me;
When I asked for him at Harar, he was towards Djibouti,
So they told me;
When I asked for him at Djibouti, he had crossed the sea,
Or so they said:
I sent to find him a hundred times,
But I never found him.
I sit by the fire and weep:
What a fool he is
To hope he will ever find anyone to equal me.

Translator: Sylvia Pankhurst

Girls' Secret Love Song

You shake the waist—we shake.
Let us shake the waist—we shake.
You shake the waist—we shake.
I am going to my lover—we shake.
Even if it is raining—we shake—
I am going to my lover—we shake.
I am going to my lover—we shake.
He is at Chesumei—we shake.
Even when night comes—we shake—
I am going to my lover—we shake.
Even if he hits me—we shake—
I am going at night—we shake.
Even if there is a wild animal—we shake—
I am going to my lover—we shake.
A person not knowing a lover—we shake—
Knows nothing at all—we shake.

Translator: J. G. Peristiany

The Worthless Lover

Trousers of wind and buttons of hail;
A lump of Shoa earth, at Gondar nothing left;
A hyena bearing meat, led on a leather thong;
Some water in a glass left standing by the fire;
A measure of water thrown on the hearth;
A horse of mist and a swollen ford;
Useless for anything, useful to no one;
Why am I in love with such a man as he?

Translator: Sylvia Pankhurst

In Honor of a King Who Acquired Several Young Wives

For me I shall buy an elderly one who will feed me,
For me I shall buy an elderly one who will feed me,
Because the young ones belong to the king.

Translators: Apolo Kagwa
Leonard Doob

HLUBI

Girl's Song

Come, it is late in the day:
All those of my age are married,
And now I wander, wander all alone.
Hold back the sun that it may not go down
Without carrying the news of my betrothal.

Translator: A. C. Jordan

ZULU

Modern Concert Song

Come here, my beloved,
Come, give me a kiss.
There is a new law
Which says we must embrace each other.
Translator: Hugh Tracey

ZIBA

Maiden's Song

I refused, of course I did,
I do not want to get married.
But father and mother compel me to,
And so I am willing to give it a try.
Translators: Hermann Rehse
Leonard Doob

YORUBA

The Trouble-Lover

Ojo is his name, Ojo the Trouble-Lover.
He loudly calls to Trouble when it's passing by,
Inviting him to come into his home and spend some time.

. . . .

True to type among the mischiefs of the Trouble-Lover's
    doing
Are these: "I will marry that girl," he says,
"I will marry her unfailingly,
No matter to whom she has already been betrothed."
He is fond of marrying wives of other men,
And so he often finds himself in hell at home.
For sometimes his stolen wives are past mistresses
In the art of domineering over husbands, of all kinds.
For instance, he once married Shango's wife,
That is, the God of Thunder's spouse,
But in his house she made him ill at ease
By belching fire from her mouth whene'er she spoke.

Translator: S. A. Babalola

"I Shall Quit"

"I shall quit.
I shall quit, I say."
This is what a woman says to threaten her husband.
The husband retorts, "I dare you to quit, if you can.
When you've gone, I will marry and bring to my house
    another wife."
Thus the man threatens the woman.
"O my husband, when you die I will die with you."
You may be sure she's still feeding in the husband's house.
She would say that the grave pit is not for two,
And that, otherwise, she would have gone with her husband
    to heaven.
It is all sheer hypocrisy on the woman's part.
You may be sure, she's still feeding in the husband's house.
No sooner is the husband dead than this Tough Lady goes
    over to another man.

Translator: S. A. Babalola

Hail Him

Hail him.
One who says and does it.
It is father.
Translator: J. H. Kwabena Nketia

Keep It Dark!

Keep it dark!
    Don't tell your wife,
    For your wife is a log
    That is smouldering surely!
Keep it dark!

Keep it dark!
    Don't tell your wife,
    For your wife is a pot
    That resounds to the breeze.
    And then "Bang!"
    It's all out and about!
Keep it dark!
        Translator: Hugh Tracey

HIMA

Song

To become a chief's favorite
Is not always comfortable;
It is like making friends
With a hippopotamus.
       Translator: Hugh Tracey

MBUNDU

Preoccupation

Chaff is in my eye,
A crocodile has me by the leg,
A goat is in the garden,
A porcupine is cooking in the pot,
Meal is drying on the pounding rock,
The King has summoned me to court,
And I must go to the funeral of my mother-in-law:
In short, I am busy.
       Translator: Merlin Ennis

The Poor Man

The poor man knows not how to eat with the rich man.
When they eat fish, he eats the head.

Invite a poor man and he rushes in
licking his lips and upsetting the plates.

The poor man has no manners, he comes along
with the blood of lice under his nails.

The face of the poor man is lined
from the hunger and thirst in his belly.

Poverty is no state fit for any mortal man.
It makes him a beast to be fed on grass.

Poverty is unjust. If it befalls a man,
though he is nobly born, he has no power with God.

Translator: Lyndon Harries

THONGA

Song of Young Men Working in the Gold Mines of Johannesburg

Stones are very hard to break
Far from home, in a foreign land,
Far from home, in a foreign land,
Stones are very hard to break.

Translator: Henri A. Junod

YORUBA

Hunger

Hunger makes a person climb up to the ceiling
And hold on to the rafters.

"I have filled my belly yesterday" does not concern hunger.
There is no God like one's throat.
We have to sacrifice daily to it.

Let the one who eats not rejoice.
Let the one who is hungry not give way to grief.
Satisfaction follows hunger.
Hunger follows satisfaction.

Translators: Bakare Gbadamosi
Ulli Beier

YORUBA

Pay Me a Visit

Song: Pay me a visit!
          Pay me a visit!
          O Money, pay me a visit!
          I'm living in this town.
Refrain: Pay me a visit!
                    Translator: S. A. Babalola

EWE

My Wings Are Plucked

My wings are plucked;—woe's the day!
Shall I ascend the tree by foot?
A buttress—that's a mother's son:
If you haven't it,
Down falls your house.
All-purpose cloth—a mother's daughter is:
If you haven't it,
You're cold-exposed.
Relations on the father side,
Relations on the mother side,
None. In whom shall I confide?
Oh, Brother!
          Translator: Geormbeeyi Adali-Mortty

The Train

The train
carries everybody
everywhere.

It carries the men
it carries the women
it carries me too
a blind boy.
Wherever it carries me
alas, I meet distress
and knock against it
with my knee.
It carries the men
it carries the women,
it carries the blind boy
to his distress.
Translator: Gerhard Kubik

The Lazy Man

When the cock crows,
the lazy man smacks his lips and says:
So it is daylight again, is it?
    before he turns over heavily.
    Translators: Bakare Gbadamosi
    Ulli Beier

YORUBA

Not Yet Enough

Now, please sing the chorus of this song with me.
"Not yet enough" are the choral words.

Solo	*Chorus*
My abuse of you will soon be enough.	Not yet enough.
Mucous are your nostrils like an old man's.	Not yet enough.
Two large wallets of flesh hang from your neck.	Not yet enough.
Because you eat broad beans voraciously,	Not yet enough.
Your cheeks are distended laterally.	Not yet enough.
Very much like those of the big bush rat.	Not yet enough.
My abuse of you will soon be enough.	Not yet enough.

It was not I who made this dainty song.
It was my friend, Ogúnrìndé of Owènà,
The son of Jósíre, who taught me that
I should never work too long on the farm
Since I am not a slave.

    Translator: S. A. Babalola

In Blowing Your Nose, You Must Expose Your Teeth

In blowing your nose, you must expose your teeth.
In stooping, one perforce exposes one's seat.
In squatting, one appears like a knock-kneed person.
It is a dozing person whose mouth becomes awry.
In looking back, one twists one's neck.

Translator: S. A. Babalola

EWE

The Sun

Where are your children, sun?
Where are your children?
As you have eaten all your own
why do you chase the moon
to take her children for your own?
You can never succeed—
go and look for your own.

Translator: Kafu Hoh

EWE

The Sky

The sky at night is like a big city
where beasts and men abound,
but never once has anyone
killed a fowl or a goat,
and no bear has ever killed a prey.
There are no accidents; there are no losses.
Everything knows its way.
Translator: Kafu Hoh

YORUBA

The Moon

The moon cannot fight
Sun leave him alone.
The moon cannot fight
Sun leave him alone!

The moon gives the earth his good light.
Come and eat beancakes with us at midnight.
Thief! Thief with the goggle eye!
Translators: Ulli Beier
Bakare Gbadamosi

A Baby Is a European

A baby is a European
he does not eat our food:
he drinks from his own water pot.

A baby is a European
he does not speak our tongue:
he is cross when the mother understands him not.

A baby is a European
he cares very little for others:
he forces his will upon his parents.

A baby is a European
he is always very sensitive:
the slightest scratch on his skin results in an ulcer.

Translator: Kafu Hoh

ZULU

Inspection

The Committee is at the school.
We are plagued by Christians.

Translator: Hugh Tracey

YORUBA

Efon (Buffalo)

When you hear thunder without rain—
It is the buffalo approaching.
We tremble at his sight.
The buffalo dies in the wildness—
And the head of the household is climbing a tree!
When a hunter meets the buffalo he will promise never to hunt again.
He will cry out and say: "I only borrowed this gun!
I only look after it for my friend!"
The buffalo is the death that makes a child climb a thorn tree!
Even the man who owns twenty horses must not attempt to pursue
An animal with such a thick skin.
An evil animal who wears a knife at the tip of his horns.
Little he cares about your hunting medicines!

Translators: Bakare Ghadamosi
Ulli Beier

AKAN

Drum Chant

(Among the Akan, certain poems are used for such purposes as heralding the movements of a chief, greeting people, announcing emergencies, and accompanying a chief drinking at a state ceremony.)

Chief they are bringing it.
They are bringing it.
They are bringing it to you.
Chief you are about to drink imported liquor.
Chief pour some on the ground.
He is sipping it slowly and gradually.
He is sipping it in little draughts.

Chief they are bringing you cool and refreshing drink.
They are bringing you palmwine.
He has got it. He is drinking it.
He has got it. He is drinking it.
He is sipping it in little draughts.
He is sipping it slowly and gradually. . . .
The residue remains. It is poured out.
Well done, Gracious one, Well done!

Translator: J. H. Kwabena Nketia

Song to the Envious

The Giver of Life
Placed the sun in great space,
And said: No hand
Shall be the length to reach it;
Though clouds disappear,
And we become a mountain,
Immovable and high,
It will not be that the hand obeys not.

The Giver of Life
Placed the sun in the heavens,
And said: No eye
Shall have the cunning to see within;
Though clouds disappear,
And we become a mountain,
Immovable and high,
It will not be that the eye obeys not.

Translator: Frances Herskovits

DINKA

War Song

Though the tribe holds a feast against me,
I shall not fear;
Though all the people hold a feast against me,
I shall not fear;
O my tribe, I am a bull with sharpened horns,
I am a maddened bull.

Translator: Godfrey Lienhardt

HOTTENTOT

Civil War Song

"Be so good, my brother,
Be so friendly,
Allow me to drink from this water hole."
"Lay down your arms
And then drink water."
"I shall not lay them down."

Translators: Leonhard Schultze
Leonard Doob

VUGUSU

Prayer of Warriors

I am sharpening my sword:
O High God, if you wish
You may give me
What you wish.
What will fall in front of me
Is what you give me.
What you do not give me
I cannot find.

Translator: Günter Wagner

FON

War Chant

The white man has brought his war to the beach.
If they look for bloody battle, they shall have it.
The amazons gather round their king and swear:
With our teeth we shall tear their throats.
Our fire drives them back to the sea.
Their priest falls victim to our war.
With their teeth the amazons tore his throat.
Oil palms are felled and come crashing down.
The white man's boat is seized in the lagoon.

Translator: Clement da Cruz

AKAN

Song for an Absent Chief

How cold is an empty room,
How sad a deserted house,
O, how melancholic is an empty room,
I roam around looking, looking.

Translator: J. H. Kwabena Nketia

AKAN

Lament

Your death has taken me by surprise.
What were your wares
that they sold out so quickly?
When I meet my father, he will hardly recognize me:
He'll find me carrying all I have:
a torn old sleeping mat and a horde of flies.
The night is fast approaching.
The orphan is dying to see its mother.

Translator: J. H. Kwabena Nketia

Praise of a Child

A child is like a rare bird.
A child is precious like coral.
A child is precious like brass.
You cannot buy a child on the market.
Not for all the money in the world.
The child you can buy for money is a slave.
We may have twenty slaves,
We may have thirty labourers,
Only a child brings us joy,
One's child is one's child.
The buttocks of our child are not so flat
That we should tie the beads on another child's hips.
One's child is one's child.
It may have a watery head or a square head,
One's child is one's child.
It is better to leave behind a child,
Than let the slaves inherit one's house.
One must not rejoice too soon over a child.
Only the one who is buried by his child,
Is the one who has truly borne a child.
On the day of our death, our hand cannot hold a single cowry.
We need a child to inherit our belongings.

Translators: Ulli Beier
Bakare Gbadamosi

Lament for the Dead Mother

Mother dear,
Mother, you freely give of what you have
fresh food and cooked meals alike.
Mother, listen to me:
the crying child will call after its mother.
Why don't you answer, Mother, when I call?
Are we quarrelling?

Translator: Geormbeeyi Adali-Mortty

Longing for Death

I have been singing, singing,
I have cried bitterly
I'm on my way.
How large this world!
Let the ferryman bring his boat
on the day of my death.
I'll wave with my left hand,
I'm on my way.
I'm on my way,
the boat of death is rocking near,
I'm on my way,
I who have sung you many songs.

Translator: P. Wiegrabe

from *The Ozidi Saga*

A Lament

"Oh Ozidi my man, my man, my man,
 my man!
Oh leader of the vanguard, my man,
 my man, my man!
Oh leader of men, my man, my man,
 my man, my man, my man,
 my man!
Oh Ozidi my man, my man, my man,
 my man!"

Translator: J. P. Clark

KUBA

Death

There is no needle without piercing point.
There is no razor without trenchant blade.
Death comes to us in many forms.

With our feet we walk the goat's earth.
With our hands we touch God's sky.
Some future day in the heat of noon,
I shall be carried shoulder high
through the village of the dead.
When I die, don't bury me under forest trees,
I fear their thorns.
When I die, don't bury me under forest trees,
I fear the dripping water.
Bury me under the great shade trees in the market,
I want to hear the drums beating
I want to feel the dancers' feet.

Translator: Ulli Beier

Prayer Before the Dead Body

The gates of the underworld are closed.
Closed are the gates.

The spirits of the dead are thronging together
like swarming mosquitoes in the evening,
like swarming mosquitoes.

Like swarms of mosquitoes dancing in the evening,
when the night has turned black, entirely black,
when the sun has sunk, has sunk below,
when the night has turned black
the mosquitoes are swarming
like whirling leaves
dead leaves in the wind.

Dead leaves in the wind,
they wait for him who will come
for him who will come and will say:
"Come" to the one and "Go" to the other.
He will say "Come" to the one and "Go" to the other
and God will be with his children.
And God will be with his children.

Translator: P. Trilles

DAHOMEAN

Dirge

I see it,
There is no enjoying beyond death.
And I say to you all,
That which your senses taste of life
Goes with you.

I say to you,
The wives you have,
The passion you know of them,
Goes with you.

I say to you,
The meats you eat,
The relish you have of them,
Goes with you.

I say to you,
The drinks you drink,
The pleasure of them,
Goes with you.

I say to you,
The pipes you smoke,
The quiet they bring,
Goes with you.

Come, then,
Dance all the colors of life
For a lover of pleasure
Now dead.

Translator: Frances Herskovits

WEST AFRICA

(in English)

GABRIEL OKARA

(Nigeria)

Spirit of the Wind

The storks are coming now—
white specks in the silent sky.
They had gone north seeking
fairer climes to build their homes
when here was raining.

They are back with me now—
Spirits of the wind,
beyond the gods' confining
hands they go north and west and east,
instinct guiding.

But willed by the gods
I'm sitting on this rock
watching them come and go
from sunrise to sundown, with the spirit
urging within.

And urging, a red pool stirs,
and each ripple is
the instinct's vital call,
desire in a million cells
confined.
O God of the gods and me,
shall I not heed
this prayer-bell call, the noon
angelus, because my stork is caged
in Singed Hair and Dark Skin?

Piano and Drums

When at break of day at a riverside
I hear jungle drums telegraphing
the mystic rhythm, urgent, raw
like bleeding flesh, speaking of
primal youth and the beginning,
I see the panther ready to pounce,
the leopard snarling about to leap
and the hunters crouch with spears poised;

And my blood ripples, turns torrent,
topples the years and at once I'm
in my mother's lap a suckling;
at once I'm walking simple
paths with no innovations,
rugged, fashioned with the naked
warmth of hurrying feet and groping hearts
in green leaves and wild flowers pulsing.

Then I hear a wailing piano
solo speaking of complex ways
in tear-furrowed concerto;
of far-away lands
and new horizons with
coaxing diminuendo, counterpoint,
crescendo. But lost in the labyrinth
of its complexities, it ends in the middle
of a phrase at a daggerpoint.

And I lost in the morning mist
of an age at a riverside keep
wandering in the mystic rhythm
of jungle drums and the concerto.

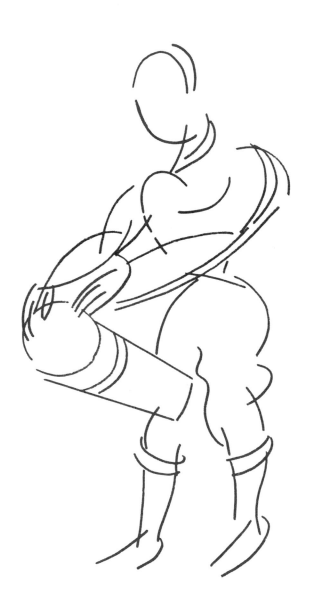

The Snow Flakes Sail Gently

The snow flakes sail gently
down from the misty eye of the sky
and fall lightly lightly on the
winter-weary elms. And the branches,
winter-stripped and nude, slowly
with the weight of the weightless snow
bow like grief-stricken mourners
as white funeral cloth is slowly
unrolled over deathless earth.
And dead sleep stealthily from the
heater rose and closed my eyes with
the touch of silk cotton on water falling.

Then I dreamed a dream
in my dead sleep. But I dreamed
not of earth dying and elms a vigil
keeping. I dreamed of birds, black
birds flying in my inside, nesting
and hatching on oil palms bearing suns
for fruits and with roots denting the
uprooters' spades. And I dreamed the
uprooters tired and limp, leaning on my roots—
their abandoned roots—
and the oil palms gave them each a sun.

But on their palms
they balanced the blinding orbs
and frowned with schisms on their
brows—for the suns reached not
the brightness of gold!

Then I awoke. I awoke
to the silently falling snow
and bent-backed elms bowing and
swaying to the winter wind like
white-robed Moslems salaaming at evening
prayer, and the earth lying inscrutable
like the face of a god in a shrine.

One Night at Victoria Beach

The wind comes rushing from the sea,
the waves curling like mambas strike
the sands and recoiling hiss in rage
washing the Aladuras' feet pressing hard
on the sand and with eyes fixed hard
on what only hearts can see, they shouting
pray, the Aladuras pray; and coming
from booths behind, compelling highlife
forces ears; and car lights startle pairs
arm in arm passing washer-words back
and forth like haggling sellers and buyers—

Still they pray, the Aladuras pray
with hands pressed against their hearts
and their white robes pressed against
their bodies by the wind; and drinking
palmwine and beer, the people boast
at bars at the beach. Still they pray.

They pray, the Aladuras pray
to what only hearts can see while dead

fishermen long dead with bones rolling
nibbled clean by nibbling fishes follow
four dead cowries shining like stars
into deep sea where fishes sit in judgment;
and living fishermen in dark huts
sit round dim lights with Babalawo
throwing their souls in four cowries
on sand, trying to see tomorrow.

Still they pray, the Aladuras pray
to what only hearts can see behind
the curling waves and the sea, the stars
and the subduing unanimity of the sky
and their white bones beneath the sand.

And standing dead on dead sands,
I felt my knees touch living sand—
but the rushing wind killed the budding words.

J. P. CLARK

(Nigeria)

Streamside Exchange

Child: River bird, river bird,
　　　Sitting all day long
　　　On hook over grass,
　　　River bird, river bird,
　　　Sing to me a song
　　　Of all that pass
　　　And say,
　　　Will mother come back today?

Bird: You cannot know
　　　And should not bother;
　　　Tide and market come and go
　　　And so shall your mother.

Night Rain

What time of night it is
I do not know
Except that like some fish
Doped out of the deep
I have bobbed up bellywise
From stream of sleep
And no cocks crow.
It is drumming hard here
And I suppose everywhere
Droning with insistent ardour upon
Our roof thatch and shed
And thro' sheaves slit open
To lightning and rafters
I can not quite make out overhead
Great water drops are dribbling
Falling like orange or mango
Fruits showered forth in the wind
Or perhaps I should say so
Much like beads I could in prayer tell
Them on string as they break
In wooden bowls and earthenware
Mother is busy now deploying
About our roomlet and floor.
Although it is so dark
I know her practised step as
She moves her bins, bags and vats
Out of the run of water
That like ants filing out of the wood
Will scatter and gain possession
Of the floor. Do not tremble then
But turn brothers, turn upon your side
Of the loosening mats

To where the others lie.
We have drunk tonight of a spell
Deeper than the owl's or bat's
That wet of wings may not fly.
Bedraggled up on the iroko, they stand
Emptied of hearts, and
Therefore will not stir, no, not
Even at dawn for then
They must scurry in to hide.
So let us roll over on our back
And again roll to the beat
Of drumming all over the land
And under its ample soothing hand
Joined to that of the sea
We will settle to sleep of the innocent and free.

Song

(References in "Song," in "Skulls and Cups," and in "Night Song" are to the tragic loss of life in the recent civil war in Nigeria.)

I can look the sun in the face
But the friends that I have lost
I dare not look at any. Yet I have held
Them all in my arms, shared with them
The same bath and bed, often
Devouring the same dish, drunk as soon
On tea as on wine, at that time
When but to think of an ill, made
By God or man, was to find
The cure prophet and physician
Did not have. Yet to look
At them now I dare not,
Though I can look the sun in the face.

Skulls and Cups

"Look, JP,
How do you tell a skull
From another?" asked Obi.
"That this, could you find where he fell,
Was Chris, that Sam, and
This there in the sand
Of course Emman. Oh yes,
How does one tell a cup on the floor
From another, when the spirit is emptied?"
And the goblets are legion,
Broken upon the fields after Nsukka.

from *Night Song*

The night for me is filled with faces,
Familiar faces no season
Of masks can cover. Often,
The strange and young I never met,
Like Nyananyo, Amangala,
Boro, all summoned from office
Or study, from sound of highlife
And sweet taste of tongues, straight into
The siren arms of war,
Intercept the faces I loved,
And sun is blotted out that I
Believe should ripen the land anew,
Though the sowing is of hearts I knew
And hold closest still in my head.
Now winds gallop through the gates
Of their eyes. In pots their mouths make
In fields already forgotten
In the fight, grow arum lilies,
Hedges of ivory about them. Let
Me but close my eyes, and they flower
Into more mornings of faces
I dare not look at,
Though I have sat it out in the sun.

CHRISTOPHER OKIGBO

(Nigeria)

Moon Mist

The stars are departed,
the sky in monocle
surveys the world under.

The stars are departed,
and I—where am I?

Stretch stretch O antennae
to clutch at this hour,
fulfilling each moment in a
broken monody.

Love Apart

The moon has ascended between us,
Between two pines
That bow to each other;

Love with the moon has ascended,
Has fed on our solitary stems;

And we are now shadows
That cling to each other,
But kiss the air only.

Watermaid

Bright
with the armpit dazzle of a lioness
she answers,
wearing white light about her;
and the waves escort her,
my lioness,
crowned with moonlight.

So brief her presence—
match-flare in wind's breath—
so brief with mirrors around me.
Downward . . .
the waves distil her:
gold crop
sinking ungathered.

Watermaid of the salt-emptiness,
grown are the ears of the secret.

For He Was a Shrub Among the Poplars

For he was a shrub among the poplars
Needing more roots
More sap to grow to sunlight
Thirsting for sunlight

A low growth among the forest.

Into the soul
The selves extended their branches
Into the moments of each living hour
Feeling for audience

Straining thin among the echoes;

And out of the solitude
Voice and soul with selves unite
Riding the echoes

Horsemen of the apocalypse

And crowned with one self
The name displays its foliage,
Hanging low

A green cloud above the forest.

from *Lament of the Drums*

They say
They will come and take away
Our drumheads
They say
They will take our drumheads
Into exile

And mangle our tendons
Puncture our membranes

They say
They will come and strip us
Of our thunder . . .

If they should come today
And ask for a praise-song

Tell them
We have tuned our raw hides
For a waking

WOLE SOYINKA

(Nigeria)

from *Idandre*

(These lines are a brief excerpt from Soyinka's memorable long
mythic poem in which he extols those gods in the Yoruba pantheon
who open the way to change and to the reconciliation of the gods
and man.)

The world was choked in wet embrace
Of serpent spawn, waiting Ajantala's rebel birth
Monster child, wrestling pachyderms of myth,

.   .   .   .

    Orisa-nla, Orunmila, Esu, Ifa were all assembled
    Defeated in the quest to fraternize with man

Wordlessly he rose, sought knowledge in the hills
Ogun the lone one saw it all, the secret
Veins of matter, and the circling lodes
Sango's spent thunderbolt served him a hammer-head
His fingers touched earth-core, and it yielded

    To think, a mere plague of finite chaos
    Stood between the gods and man

.   .   .   .

He made a mesh of elements, from stone
Of fire in earthfruit, the womb of energies
He made an anvil of the peaks, and kneaded
Red clay for his mould. In his hand the Weapon
Gleamed, born of the primal mechanic

    And this pledge he gave the heavens
    I will clear a path to man

．　．　．　．
    may we celebrate the stray electron, defiant
Of patterns, celebrate the splitting of the gods
Canonization of the strong hand of a slave who set
The rock in revolution—

All hail Saint Atunda, First revolutionary
Grand iconoclast at genesis.

Season

    Rust is ripeness, rust,
    And the wilted corn-plume.
    Pollen is mating-time when swallows
    Weave a dance
    Of feathered arrows
    Thread corn-stalks in winged
    Streaks of light. And we loved to hear
    Spliced phrases of the wind, to hear
    Rasps in the field, where corn-leaves
    Pierce like bamboo slivers.

    Now, garnerers we,
    Awaiting rust on tassels, draw
    Long shadows from the dusk, wreathe
    The thatch in wood-smoke. Laden stalks
    Ride the germ's decay—we await
    The promise of the rust.

Ancestral Faces

They sneaked into the limbo of time,
But could not muffle the gay jingling
Bells on the frothy necks
Of the sacrificial sheep
That limped and nodded after them.
They could not hide the moss on the bald pate
Of their reverent heads,
And the gnarled bark of the wawa tree;
Nor the rust on the ancient state-swords
Nor the skulls studded with grinning cowries.
They could not silence the drums,
The fibre of their souls and ours—
The drums that whisper to us behind black sinewy
    hands.
They gazed and
Sweeping like white locusts through the forests
Saw the same men, slightly wizened,
Shuffle their sandalled feet to the same rhythms.
They heard the same words of wisdom uttered
Between puffs of pale blue smoke.
They saw us,
And said! They have not changed!

The Dry Season

The year is withering; the wind
Blows down the leaves;
Men stand under eaves
And overhear the secrets
Of the cold dry wind,
Of the half-bare trees.

The grasses are tall and tinted,
Straw-gold hues of dryness,
And the contradicting awryness,
Of the dusty roads a-scatter
With pools of colourful leaves,
With ghosts of the dreaming year.

And soon, soon the fires,
The fires will begin to burn,
The hawk will flutter and turn
On its wings and swoop for the mouse,
The dogs will run for the hare,
The hare for its little life.

The Mesh

We have come to the cross-roads
And I must either leave or come with you.
I lingered over the choice
But in the darkness of my doubts
You lifted the lamp of love
And I saw in your face
The road that I should take.

MABEL SEGUN

(Nigeria)

Conflict

Here we stand
infants overblown,
poised between two civilisations,
finding the balance irksome,
itching for something to happen,
to tip us one way or the other,
groping in the dark for a helping hand
and finding none.
I'm tired, O my God, I'm tired,
I'm tired of hanging in the middle way—
but where can I go?

The Pigeon-Hole

How I wish I could pigeon-hole myself
and neatly fix a label on!
But self-knowledge comes too late
and by the time I've known myself
I am no longer what I was.

I knew a woman once
who had a delinquent child.
She never had a moment's peace of mind
waiting in constant fear,

listening for the dreaded knock
and the cold tones of policeman:
"Madam, you're wanted at the station."
I don't know if the knock ever came
but she feared on right till
we moved away from the street.
She used to say,
"It's the uncertainty that worries me—
if only I knew for certain . . ."

If only I knew for certain
what my delinquent self would do . . .
But I never know
until the deed is done
and I live on fearing,
wondering which part of me will be supreme—
the old and tested one, the present
or the future unknown.
Sometimes all three have equal power
and then
how I long for a pigeon-hole.

JOE DE GRAFT

(Ghana)

The Avenue: N.Y. City

Shapes of men
     Caught-riveted spread-eagle-wise
     In toils of steel girders
     Scraping skywards into the sun.

Souls of men
     Trapped-lost blind-mouse-like
     In a maze of asphalt channels,
     Rat-racing round the clock

Man
     The city builder
Man
     The world girdler
Man
     The rejected prayer.

JOHN EKWERE

(Nigeria)

Rejoinder

Now no more the paleface strangers
With unhallowed feet
The heritage of our fathers profane;
Now no missioned benevolent despots
Bull-doze an unwilling race;
No more now the foreign hawks
On alien chickens prey—
But we on us!

MBELLA SONNE DIPOKO

(Cameroon)

Our History

To pre-colonial Africa

And the waves arrived
Swimming in like hump-backed divers
With their finds from far-away seas.

Their lustre gave the illusion of pearls
As shorewards they shoved up mighty canoes
And looked like the carcass of drifting whales.

And our sight misled us
When the sun's glint on the spear's blade
Passed for lightning

And the gun-fire of conquest
The thunderbolt that razed the forest.

So did our days change their garb
From hides of leopard skin
To prints of false lions
That fall in tatters
Like the wings of whipped butterflies.

Pain

All was quiet in this park
Until the wind, like a gasping monster, announced
The tyrant's coming.
Then did the branches talk in agony.

You remember that raging storm?

In their fear despairing flowers nevertheless held
    bouquets to the grim king;

Meteors were the tassels of his crown
While like branches that only spoke when the storm
    menaced
We cried in agony as we fell
Slashed by the cold blade of an invisible sword.

Mutilated, our limbs were swept away by the rain
But not our blood;
Indelible, it stuck on the walls
Like wild gum on tree-trunks.

DENNIS OSADEBAY

(Nigeria)

Young Africa's Plea

Don't preserve my customs
As some fine curios
To suit some white historian's tastes.
There's nothing artificial
That beats the natural way,
In culture and ideals of life.
Let me play with the white man's ways.
Let me work with the black man's brains,
Let my affairs sort themselves out.
Then in sweet re-birth
I'll rise a better man,
Not ashamed to face the world.
Those who doubt my talents
In secret fear my strength;
They know I am no less a man.
Let them bury their prejudice,
Let them show their noble sides,
Let me have untrammelled growth.
My friends will never know regret
And I, I never once forget.

KEN TSARO-WIWA

(Nigeria)

Night Encounter

Coming up the stairs
Through the light drizzle
One dark night, I met him
One with the darkness
I stopped for a moment.
Frighted, tense.

He laughed gently and I relaxed
Happy to find
In spite of the gun
He was still a man.

It lit the dark
That gentle laugh
In the pith of night . . .

Deeper that night
The skies wept heavy tears
But I heard only the low laugh
Of the soldier on patrol duty
The man who was about to die.

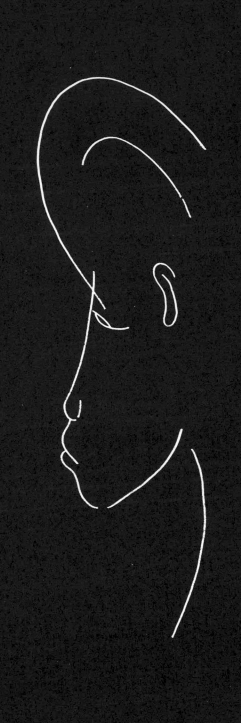

Voices

They speak of taxes
Of oil and power

They speak of honour
And pride of tribe

They speak of war
Of bows and arrows

They speak of tanks
And putrid human flesh

I sing my love
For Maria.

AIG HIGO

(Nigeria)

Myself My Slogan

My background is working class
My foreground is working class
I am myself my slogan
Eat, booze and be married
For tomorrow we vote.

OKOGBULE WONODI

(Nigeria)

Lament of the Exiles

I hear the cooing music of doves
And the talk of fading love
Among the men of God. I see the exiles
Returning, spotless, with kola-free teeth.

They return and dance at market places
And there are no drums for their waists;
The masquerades have all married
and gone home. Only the exiles dance . . .

I fear the rush of harmattan dust
I fear the gradual wearing of the riverbanks
And the benign whisper of still voices
Saying: "Return to Kano, O man of the people."

O my brothers, let me walk alone this evening
Among the mangroves and search for love
Brought by sea-surfs. Let me lie with the naked
And feel their cold in my spine.

The Immigrant

Flying over Chicago that night he saw
America as through a telescope
With a multiple of eyes; and her streets,
Straight-eyed, blinked, bidding and binding his eyes.

He tried another look, this time sideways,
Flapping his eyelids close to the window
And his mouth, like clams at fulltide, opened full.
He saw nothing but distant specks of stars
Piercing like arrows the darkness beyond.

But beyond he saw ten dainty maidens
And beside them ten young men in loincloths
And he brought the sacred drums and drumsticks
And walked before them; and the maidens
And the young men gave their waists to the drum
And his voice dug deep into the Fathers.
They danced behind him, frenzied as prophets.
Sweating, beating a staccato of sounds,
He was one with them, lost to the moment.

"This is O'Hare"
                    and the dancers sank
fast over fast-running pillars of light.

KOFI AWOONOR

(Ghana)

from *Songs of Sorrow*

Something has happened to me
The things so great that I cannot weep;
I have no sons to fire the gun when I die
And no daughters to wail when I close my mouth
I have wandered on the wilderness
The great wilderness men call life
The rain has beaten me,
And the sharp stumps cut as keen as knives
I shall go beyond and rest.
I have no kin and no brother,
Death has made war upon our house.

R. E. G. ARMATTOE

(Ghana)

The Lonely Soul

I met an old woman
   Talking by herself
Down a lonely road.
   Talking to herself,
Laughing all the time,
   Talking to herself
Down a country road.
Child, you cannot know
Why folks talk alone.
If the road be long
And travellers none,
   A man talks to himself.
If showers of sorrows
Fall down like arrows
The lone wayfarer
   May talk by himself.
So an old woman
On lone country roads,
Laughing all the time,
   May babble to herself
To keep the tears away.
Woman, you are sad!
'Tis the same with me.

TSEGAYE GABRE-MEDHIN

(Ethiopia)

from *Oda Oak Oracle*

It is not easy, Ukutee,
To speak
Of the gloomy path
Of a lone walker.
Loneliness is
When the ripe fruit fails
To make the bird
Aware of its existence.
Loneliness is
When the avoided heart,
Growing stale every night,
Wears a mask of bitterness,
While the tense veins
Growing frantic and mad
Scratch at the mask
Of a stricken heart.
Loneliness is
When the aged mule
Rubs its flank
Against the deserted trunk
Of a dead bush.
Loneliness is
When the moon is left cold
Among a glowing
Jungle of stars.

CHINUA ACHEBE

(Nigeria)

Question

Angled sunbeam lowered
like Jacob's ladder through
sky's peep-hole pierced in the roof
to my silent floor and bared feet.
Are these your creatures
these crowding specks
stomping your lighted corridor
to a remote sun, like doped
acrobatic angels gyrating
at needlepoint to divert a high
unamused god? Or am I
sole stranger in a twilight room
I called my own overrun
and possessed long ago by myriads more
as yet invisible in all
this surrounding penumbra?

UCHE OKEKE

(Nigeria)

The Home of Images

I shall return to the home of images:
I shall go back to the city of ruins:
I shall return to honour the Oba,
his court and his all;
I shall return
the lone light in the city of the night—
sad, solemn, solitary star in dark domain;
there shall I be
image of time in timeless sphere
Life longs for life for light,
and I long to flame yellow in my desolate grey:
I shall learn to live and be lost
I shall learn to be lonely, to be forgotten—
to die and remain granite-grey.
I shall return to the graven people;
I shall go back to the city of darkness:
I must know how to feel lost,
how to live lonely among grey granite people;
I shall return to the home of images—
the home of long forgotten folk.

WEST AFRICA

(translated from the French)

LÉOPOLD SÉDAR SENGHOR

(Senegal)

Black Woman

Naked woman, black woman
Clothed with your colour which is life, with your form
which is beauty!
In your shadow I have grown up; the gentleness of your
hands was laid over my eyes
And now, high up on the sun-baked pass, at the heart of
summer, at the heart of noon, I come upon you, my
Promised Land,
And your beauty strikes me to the heart like the flash of an
eagle.

Naked woman, dark woman
Firm-fleshed ripe fruit, sombre raptures of black wine, mouth
making lyrical my mouth
Savannah stretching to clear horizons, savannah shuddering
beneath the East Wind's eager caresses
Carved tom-tom, taut tom-tom, muttering under the Con-
queror's fingers
Your solemn contralto voice is the spiritual song of the
Beloved.

Naked woman, dark woman
Oil that no breath ruffles, calm oil on the athlete's flanks, on
the flanks of the Princes of Mali
Gazelle limbed in Paradise, pearls are stars on the night of
your skin

Delights of the mind, the glinting of red gold against your
    watered skin
Under the shadow of your hair, my care is lightened by the
    neighbouring suns of your eyes. ·

Naked woman, black woman
I sing your beauty that passes, the form that I fix in the
    Eternal,
Before jealous Fate turn you to ashes to feed the roots of life.

Translators: John Reed
Clive Wake

Night of Sine

Woman, lay on my forehead your perfumed hands, hands softer
    than fur.
Above, the swaying palm trees rustle in the high night breeze
Hardly at all. No lullaby even.
The rhythmic silence cradles us.
Listen to its song, listen to our dark blood beat, listen
To the deep pulse of Africa beating in the mist of forgotten villages.

See the tired moon comes down to her bed on the slack sea
The laughter grows weary, the story-tellers even
Are nodding their heads like a child on the back of its mother
The feet of the dancers grow heavy, and heavy the voice of the an-
    swering choirs.

It is the hour of stars, of Night that dreams
Leaning upon this hill of clouds, wrapped in its long milky cloth.

The roofs of the huts gleam tenderly. What do they say so secretly
to the stars?
Inside the fire goes out among intimate smells that are acrid and
sweet.

Woman, light the clear oil lamp, where the ancestors gathered
around may talk as parents talk when the children are put to
bed.
Listen to the voice of the ancients of Elissa. Exiled like us
They have never wanted to die, to let the torrent of their seed be
lost in the sands.
Let me listen in the smoky hut where there comes a glimpse of the
friendly spirits
My head on your bosom warm like a *dang* still steaming from the
fire.
Let me breathe the smell of our Dead, gather and speak out again
their living voice, learn to
Live before I go down, deeper than diver, into the high profundities
of sleep.

Translators: John Reed
Clive Wake

from *Chaka*

Chaka:

(He has closed his eyes for a moment. He opens them and for a long time stares towards the East, his solemn face radiant.)

The night is coming. My lovely Night the moon a golden coin.
I hear the cooing of Noliwe in the morning, the cinnamon apple
    that rolls in the scented grass.

Chorus:

He is leaving us. How black he is. It is the time of loneliness.
Let us sing the Zulu, let our voices comfort him.
Bayete Baba! Bayete O Zulu!

Leader of the Chorus:

How splendid he is. It is the time of re-birth.
The poem is ripe in the garden of childhood, it is time for love.

Translators: John Reed
Clive Wake

Joal

Joal!
I remember

I remember the *signares** in the green shadow of the verandas
Signares with eyes surreal as moonlight on the beach.

I remember the pomps of sunset
That Kumba N'Dofene wanted cut to make his royal cloak.

I remember the funeral feasts, smoking with the blood of slaughtered cattle
With the noise of quarrels and the *griot's*** rhapsodies.

I remember pagan rhythmic singing of the *Tantum Ergo*
And processions and palms and triumphal arches.

I remember the dance of the girls who are ready for marriage
The choruses at the wrestling . . . oh! the young men in the final dance bodies
Bent forward, slender and the women's pure shout of love
. . . *Kor Siga!*

I remember, I remember . . .
In my head the rhythm of the tramp tramp
So wearily down the days of Europe where there comes,
Now and then a little orphaned jazz that goes sobbing, sobbing, sobbing.

Translators: John Reed
Clive Wake

---

* A class of women whose elevated status is based largely on their role in trade.

** The term *griot* is not readily defined. He is a poet, bard, historian, who is spokesman and recorder of the history and traditions of his people, often in the service of a particular ruler.

Prayer to Masks

MASKS! Masks!
Black mask red mask, you white-and-black masks
Masks of the four points from which the Spirit blows
In silence I salute you!
Nor you the least, Lion-headed Ancestor
You guard this place forbidden to all laughter of women, to all
smiles that fade
You distill this air of eternity in which I breathe the air of my
Fathers.
Masks of unmasked faces, stripped of the marks of illness and the
lines of age
You who have fashioned this portrait, this my face bent over the
altar of white paper
In your own image, hear me!
The Africa of the empires is dying: see the agony of a pitiful prin-
cess
And Europe too where we are joined by the navel.
Fix your unchanging eyes upon your children, who are given orders
Who give away their lives like the poor their last clothes.
Let us report present at the rebirth of the World
Like the yeast which white flour needs.
For who would teach rhythm to a dead world of machines and guns?
Who would give the cry of joy to wake the dead and the bereaved
at dawn?
Say, who would give back the memory of life to the man whose
hopes are smashed?
They call us men of coffee cotton oil
They call us men of death.
We are the men of the dance, whose feet draw new strength pound-
ing the hardened earth.

Translators: John Reed
Clive Wake

from *For Koras and Balafong*

Toko'Waly my uncle, do you remember those distant nights when
    my head grew heavy against the patience of your back?
Or holding me by the hand, your hand led me through the shadows
    and signs?
The fields are flowers of glow worms; the stars come to rest on the
    grass, on the trees.
All around is silence.
Only the droning scents of the bush, hives of red bees drowning the
    stridulation of the crickets
And the muffled tom-tom, the far-off breathing of the night.
But you, Toko'Waly, hear what is beyond hearing
You explain to me the signs that the Ancestors give in the calm seas
    of the constellations
The Bull the Scorpion the Leopard, the Elephant the familiar Fishes
And the milky ceremony of the Spirits along the unending shores of
    heaven.
And now see the wisdom of the moon-goddess, see the veils of the
    shadows fall.
African night my black night, mystical-lucid black-brilliant
You rest at one with the earth, you are the earth and the harmonious
    hills.
O classic Beauty that is never angular, but subtle slender soaring
    line!
O classic face! From the rounded forehead under the odorous forest
    and the wide oblique eyes down to the gracious bay of the chin
    and
The impetuous leap of the twin hills! Curves of gentleness melodi-
    ous face.

O my Lioness my dark Beauty, my black Night my Black One my
   Naked One!
How often have you made my heart beat like the unconquered
   leopard in his narrow cage.
Night delivering me from arguments and sophistries of salons,
   from pirouetting pretexts, from calculated hatred and humane
   butchery

Night dissolving all my contradictions, all contradictions in the first
   unity of your blackness
Take the child who is still a child, that twelve wandering years have
   not made old.
I bring from Europe only this friend, her child's eyes bright among
   the Breton mists.

Translators: John Reed
Clive Wake

Long, Long You Have Held Between Your Hands

[*For khalam*]

Long, long you have held between your hands the black face of the
    warrior
Held as if already there fell on it a twilight of death.
From the hill I have seen the sun set in the bays of your eyes.
When shall I see again, my country, the pure horizon of your face?
When shall I sit down once more at the dark table of your breast?

Hidden in the half-darkness, the nest of gentle words.

I shall see other skies and other eyes
I shall drink at the spring of other mouths cooler than lemons
I shall sleep under the roof of other heads of hair in shelter from
    storms.
But every year, when the rum of springtime sets my memory ablaze
I shall be full of regret for my homeland and the rain from your
    eyes on the thirsty savannahs.

Translators: John Reed
Clive Wake

New York

Jazz orchestra: solo trumpet

1.

NEW YORK! At first your beauty confused me, and your great long-
legged golden girls.
I was so timid at first under your blue metallic eyes, your frosty smile
So timid. And the disquiet in the depth of your skyscraper streets
Lifting up owl eyes in the sun's eclipse.
Your sulphurous light and the livid shafts (their heads dumbfound-
ing the sky)
Skyscrapers defying cyclones on their muscles of steel and their
weathered stone skins.
But a fortnight on the bald sidewalks of Manhattan
—At the end of the third week the fever takes you with the pounce
of a jaguar
A fortnight with no well or pasture, all the birds of the air
Fall suddenly dead below the high ashes of the terraces.
No child's laughter blossoms, his hand in my fresh hand
No mother's breast. Legs in nylon. Legs and breasts with no sweat
and no smell.
No tender word for mouths are lipless. Hard cash buys artificial
hearts.
No book where wisdom is read. The painter's palette flowers with
crystals of coral.
Insomniac nights O nights of Manhattan, tormented by fatuous fires,
while the klaxons cry through the empty hours
And dark waters bear away hygienic loves, like the bodies of chil-
dren on a river in flood.

2.

It is the time of signs and reckonings
New York! It is the time of manna and hyssop.
Only listen to God's trombones, your heart beating to the rhythm of
blood your blood.
I have seen Harlem humming with sounds and solemn colour and
flamboyant smells
—(It is tea-time for the man who delivers pharmaceutical products)
I have seen them preparing at flight of day, the festival of the Night.
I proclaim there is more truth in the Night than in the day.
It is the pure hour when God sets the life before memory germinat-
ing in the streets
All the amphibious elements shining like suns.
Harlem Harlem! I have seen Harlem Harlem! A breeze green with
corn springing from the pavements ploughed by the bare feet
of dancers in
Crests and waves of silk and breasts of spearheads, ballets of lilies
and fabulous masks
The mangoes of love roll from the low houses under the police
horses' hooves.
I have seen down the sidewalks streams of white rum and streams of
black milk in the blue haze of cigars.
I have seen the sky at evening snowing cotton flowers and wings of
seraphim and wizard's plumes.
Listen, New York, listen to your brazen male voice your vibrant
oboe voice, the muted anguish of your tears falling in great
clots of blood
Listen to the far beating of your nocturnal heart, rhythm and blood
of the drum, drum and blood and drum.

3.

New York! I say to New York, let the black blood flow into your
    blood
Cleaning the rust from your steel articulations, like an oil of life
Giving your bridges the curve of the hills, the liana's suppleness.
See, the ancient times come again, unity is rediscovered the recon-
    ciliation of the Lion the Bull and the Tree
The idea is linked to the act the ear to the heart the sign to the sense.
See your rivers murmuring with musky caymans, manatees with eyes
    of mirage. There is no need to invent the Mermaids.
It is enough to open your eyes to the April rainbow
And the ears, above all the ears to God who with a burst of saxo-
    phone laughter created the heavens and the earth in six days.
And on the seventh day, he slept his great negro sleep.

Translators: John Reed
Clive Wake

DAVID DIOP

(Senegal)

The Renegade

My brother you flash your teeth in response to every hypocrisy
My brother with gold-rimmed glasses
You give your master a blue-eyed faithful look
My poor brother in immaculate evening dress
Screaming and whispering and pleading in the parlours of
    condescension
We pity you
Your country's burning sun is nothing but a shadow
On your serene "civilized" brow
And the thought of your grandmother's hut
Brings blushes to your face that is bleached
By years of humiliation and bad conscience
And while you trample on the bitter red soil of Africa
Let these words of anguish keep time with your restless step—
O I am lonely so lonely here.

Translator: Sangodare Akanji

Africa

Africa my Africa
Africa of proud warriors in the ancestral savannahs
Africa my grandmother sings of
Beside her distant river
I have never seen you
But my gaze is full of your blood
Your black blood spilt over the fields
The blood of your sweat
The sweat of your toil
The toil of slavery
The slavery of your children
Africa, tell me Africa,
Are you the back that bends
Lies down under the weight of humbleness?
The trembling back striped red
That says yes to the sjambok on the roads of noon?
Solemnly a voice answers me
"Impetuous child, that young and sturdy tree
That tree that grows
There splendidly alone among white and faded flowers
Is Africa, your Africa. It puts forth new shoots
With patience and stubbornness puts forth new shoots
Slowly its fruits grow to have
The bitter taste of liberty."

Translator: Ulli Beier

Rama Kam

Ah, your slow and brutal stare
Your lips, yes, the flavor of the mango
    Rama Kam
Your flesh the ripe black fruit
That moves my soul to sing
    Rama Kam
When you walk by, the loveliest
    are devoured by jealousy
    before the rhythmic witness of your hips
    Rama Kam
When you dance
The tom-tom Rama Kam
The tom-tom taut like the conquering passion of the lover
Gasping under the bounding fingers of the drummer
When you love
When you love Rama Kam
It is the thunder trembling
In the night of your flesh the lightning flash
Leaving me full of the breath of you O
    Rama Kam!

Translator: Samuel Allen

Defiance Against Force

You who bow you who mourn
You who die one day like that without knowing why
You who struggle, who sit up and watch so the Other can rest
You who no longer look with laughter in your eyes
You my brother with the face of fear and anguish
    Rise up and shout: NO!

Translator: Clive Wake

BIRAGO DIOP

(Senegal)

Souffles

(*It is the breath of the ancestors*)

Listen more often to things than to beings
    Hear the fire's voice,
    Hear the voice of water.
    Hear, in the wind, the sobbing of the trees.
It is the breath of the ancestors.

The dead are not gone forever
They are in the paling shadows,
They are in the darkening shadows.

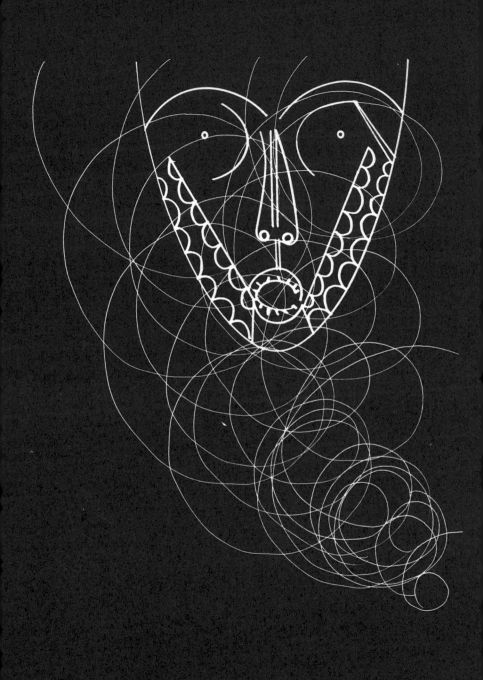

The dead are not beneath the ground,
They are in the rustling tree,
In the murmuring wood,
The flowing water,
The still water,
In the lonely place, in the crowd;
The dead are never dead.

Listen more often to things than to beings.
Hear the fire's voice.
Hear the voice of water.
In the wind hear the sobbing of the trees.
It is the breath of the ancestors.
They are not gone
They are not beneath the ground
They are not dead.

The dead are not gone forever.
They are in a woman's breast,
A child's cry, a glowing ember.
The dead are not beneath the earth,
They are in the flickering fire,
In the weeping plant, the groaning rock,
The wooded place, the home.
The dead are never dead.

Listen more often to things than to beings
Hear the fire's voice,
Hear the voice of water.
Hear, in the wind, the sobbing of the trees.
It is the breath of the ancestors.

Translator: Samuel Allen

IBRA DIAW

(Senegal)

I Shall Bring Honour to My Blood

I shall bring honour to my blood
I shall not draw back nor falter
The meaning of my life,
to leave my blood without a blemish
if I draw back
thou great ancestor that regardest me
from the depths of thy tomb
strike me with thy age-old hand.

Translator: Lamine Diakhaté

TCHICAYA U TAM'SI

(Congo-Brazzaville)

from *The Belly Remains*

Of course the belly remains pure
under a treasure of white bones
next opened to the song of a warrior
lost with all hands
in the flames of his passion

.   .   .   .

Of course, the belly remains.
Is it more soiled than pure?
Because of certain heart fragments?
Love for love
is as distressing as the rest.
But love for life

the one that is given from the belly
earth takes it in hand
Thank God prophets fall
more often on the back
more often arms wide open
more often
the belly facing the sky!
                Translator: Edouard J. Maunick

from *Cradlesong*

—I love you my child
sleep if you love your mother

—Woman does the child sleep well

—He sleeps well
the moths dance in ellipse
about his head

—If he sleeps well then do not weep

—He sleeps well
the moths dance in ellipse
about his head

                Translator: Gerald Moore

from *Obolus*

My mother lies a body before me
My hands are her death mask
my hands bear the lines of her face
my hands have her flexible sadness
my hands have their palms in her mouth

. . . .

Were you among the hay my mother

there is no mark of love on my body
whence did you come when I came within you
abstraction of solitude

I see through you the desert behind appearances

I feel through you the guilty nakedness of soft waters

Do we know that the roses bloom
at the fringes of our clinical birth

I can console you
I can cure you
I can betray you

I can rock you

Translator: Gerald Moore

Marine Nocturne

Tell me
what makes the sea grey
what makes the sea full
from whom does it take its madness

who will tie the waves and tears
together?

Translator: Gerald Moore

Bow Harp

Life
like a gendarme's baton
pointing the direction
of the bad road

Translator: Gerald Moore

(Mali)

from *Requiem for a Black Girl*

What have you done with my letters
Tell me
What have you done with my dreams
Speak to me!

What did you say when there was nothing
    I could say

Speak
What did you think when I cried out to you
Speak to me!

Oh how I loved you
Yes
Now I have killed you in me
Yes . . .
    . . . it is true.

Always the stronger—you
Always more loving—
    me.

  . . . .
What have you done with my letters
Speak
What have you done with my dreams
Speak to me!

Translator: Samuel Allen

CAMARA LAYE

(Guinea)

To My Mother

Black woman, African woman, O my mother, I think of you . . .

O Dâman, mother, you who bore me on your back, who
nursed me, guided my first steps, you who were the first
to make me see the wonders of the world, I think of you . . .

Woman of the fields, woman of the streams, woman of the
great river, O my mother, I think of you . . .

O Dâman, you my mother, you who dried my tears, who cheered
my heart, you who would patiently indulge my whims, how I
would love to be close by your side once more, to be a child
close by your side!

Simple woman, woman of resignation, O my mother, I
think of you . . .

O Dâman, Dâman of the great blacksmith clan, my thought
keeps turning back to you, yours keeps me company with
every step, O Dâman, my mother, how I would love to be
within your warmth once more, to be a child close by your
side . . .

Black woman, African woman, O my mother, I give thanks;
thanks for everything you did for me, your son, so far, so close
to you!

Translator: Norman R. Shapiro

SOUTH AFRICA

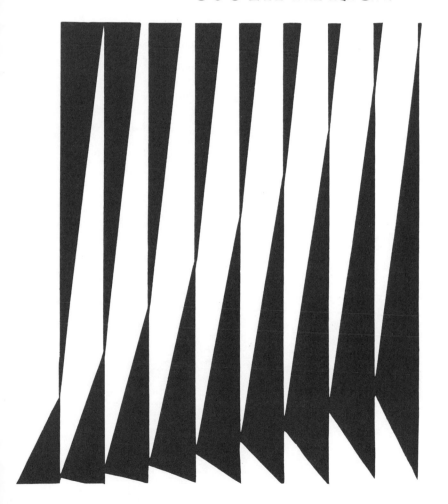

A Zulu Lyric

(Republic of South Africa)

Take off your hat.
What is your home name?
Who is your father?
Who is your chief?
Where do you pay your tax?
What river do you drink?
We mourn for our country.
Translator: Hugh Tracey

L. D. RADITLADI

(Botswana)

Motswasele's Farewell

(Motswasele II was a chief of the Kwena tribe of what is now Botswana. Some of his tribe rose against him, and here we see him shortly before the battle in which he is killed and his forces defeated.)

Is this my country or is it mere soil
Which I must lick with my tongue?
Is this the seat where I must
Rest when banished from the stool
Of chieftainship, in this my country?
Must I live outlawed like a lone beast of prey,
Far, far, from the homage of my people?
Farewell green fields of my home,

I bow my head to you, terrors of this place.
I bow my head to you, O country of despair.
And you our great enemy, you O death,
Receive me into that vast domain of yours.
The fortunes of earth have shunned and escaped me
But life there perchance will free me from torment.
I beseech you approach me, O death, I desire you!
Open O grave, and receive me, I come!
Release me from this world, O spear, I am weary!

Translator: D. T. Cole
Adapted by Peggy Rutherfoord

B. W. VILAKAZI

(Republic of South Africa)

from *Umamina*

1.

Come Mamina,
When you did gaze on me, ebony maiden,
I knew not whither I would go,
My knees quivered, my weapons dropped,
I was filled with the bitterness that lurks in the heart
Like a wild beast, and is called love.

Alas, I seek you, Mamina,
You have hidden in the fields of dry grass.
The dry grass is my soul,
Yet you are loitering there,
Gathering blackberries, herbs and creepers.

2.

Your love and mine, O Mamina,
Excel the mind, beyond the power of the diviners,

. . . .

"Are you not one of the ancestral spirits"?
Perchance you have lost your way,
On your journey to the gates of Heaven,
And have branched off to Earth
And chanced on the roots of love.

3.

Come Mamina,
You are the star of my soul
You alone are in the depth of my veins
Which make my heart tremble.
You are like the track of the field rat
Which winds through old grass and heads far off.

4.

Come Mamina,
I feel loneliness steal over me.
This earth affords no refuge for me.
Come and lead me to your land, Mamina.
There let us solve the mystery of this love,
That I may know it, Mamina;
Know it wholly with the spirit of the ancestors.

Translator: R. M. Mfeka
Adapted by Peggy Rutherfoord

DENNIS BRUTUS

(Republic of South Africa)

from *Poem*

Somehow we survive
and tenderness, frustrated, does not wither.

Investigating searchlights rake
our naked unprotected contours;

. . . .

boots club on the peeling door.

But somehow we survive
severance, deprivation, loss.

Patrols uncoil along the asphalt dark
hissing their menace to our lives,

most cruel, all our land is scarred with terror,
rendered unlovely and unlovable;
sundered are we and all our passionate surrender

but somehow tenderness survives.

Nightsong City

Sleep well, my love, sleep well:
the harbour lights glaze over restless docks,
police cars cockroach through the tunnel streets;

from the shanties creaking iron-sheets
violence like a bug-infested rag is tossed
and fear is immanent as sound in the wind-swung bell;

the long day's anger pants from sand and rocks;
but for this breathing night at least,
my land, my love, sleep well.

The sounds begin again:
the siren in the night
the thunder at the door
the shriek of nerves in pain.

Then the keening crescendo
of faces split by pain
the wordless, endless wail
only the unfree know.

Importunate as rain
the wraiths exhale their woe
over the sirens, knuckles, boots;
my sounds begin again.

F. M. MULIKITA

(Republic of South Africa)

from *Shaka Zulu*

Shaka was the Great Elephant who stamped his
enemies to dust. He was the Lion of Lions who
gobbled up the sons of Zwide. The Thunder of Zulu
in Heaven sounded throughout the land. He sent
Ntombazi the skull-gatherer to the hyenas. He
smelled out the bloodstench of Nobela the Witch.
He united the warring tribes of Nguniland to build
the greatest empire Africa had ever known. You
will see Shaka planning to turn the Zulu nation from
soldiers into citizens. But history shrugs off the
power of kings, and you will see the beginning of the
sadness that comes to all great men who thought
they knew the answers to life but then realize they
do not even understand the questions. But I am
speaking ahead of myself. Watch King Shaka now
in the days of his glory.

MONGAMELI MABONA

(Republic of South Africa)

The Sea

Ocean,
Green or blue or iron-gray,
As the light
Strikes you.
Primordial flood,
Relentless and remorseless
Like a woman in a rage.
My dark desire, silent
Grave of my hopes;
You witch, you sorceress!
I saw your burning gold—

Yesterday,
As the sun rose,
But was not deceived,
For I have tasted
Your bitter brine,
Cold grave of my fathers,
As they were brought
In galleyfuls
To far-off hells.
O shifting, treacherous,
Beautiful, furious!
What scandalous passions
Have you aroused
With your sinuous motions—
Tempting
The golden sun?

What murderous lies
Have you told the keen winds,
Your blue dragon belly
Full of white bones
Of Africa's princes
From Guinea, Congo,
And Angola?
I panic
At your artful
Insouciance,
At the careless exposure
Of your plenteous curves,
Beautiful ocean!
Obscene power of life,
Sombre grave of my fathers.

MAZISI KUNENE

(Republic of South Africa)

As Long as I Live

When I still can remember
When I still have eyes to see
When I still have hands to hold
When I still have feet to drag
So long shall I bear your name with all the days
So long shall I stare at you with all the stars of heaven
Though you lead me to their sadistic beasts
I shall find a way to give my burden-love
Blaming your careless truths on yesterdays.
Because I swear by life herself
When you still live, so shall I live
Turning the night into day, forcing her
To make you lie pompous on its pathways.
So shall I wander around the rim of the sun
Till her being attains your fullness
As long as I live . . .

Farewell

O beloved farewell . . .
Hold these leaping dreams of fire
With the skeletal hands of death
So that when hungry night encroaches
You defy her stubborn intrigues.

Do not look to where we turn and seethe
We pale humanity, like worms
(The ululations might bind you to our grief)
Whose feet carry the duty of life.

Farewell beloved
Even the hush that haunts the afternoon
Will sing the ding-dong drum of your ultimate joy
Where we sit by the fireside tossing the memories
Making the parts fit into each day complete;
Yet knowing ours is a return of emptiness
Farewell, yewu . . . ye.

EAST AFRICA

Y. S. CHEMBA

(Uganda)

My Newest Bride

They came in hordes singing her name,
Voices grew hoarse praising her beauty,
Her charm was beyond all compare,
Her soft touch soothed all pain,
Her words taught all wisdom,
And her embrace brought eternal bliss.

Moved to fever pitch I swore,
I swore before the gathered village,
I swore on the bones of my forefathers,
That I would neither sleep nor rest,
Until she was my wife, my betrothed.

It was a fever, as virulent a fever as you ever saw,
For I ask you my friends, my brothers,
Know you of any fool,
Who paid the bride price I paid,
Not ever having set eyes on the girl?

And what a bride price!
Facing Greener guns with stones,
Long prison sentences without trial,
Hunger strikes, deportation, the lot!
But I paid, I paid every cent of it.

At last she came, she came my bride!
The drums throbbed, they throbbed for a week,
The village sang and drank,

We danced and laughed,
And drank and laughed and danced again.

She was beautiful beyond compare,
Her sparkling eyes,
Her firm warm breasts,
Her beautiful smile and merry laughter,
Spelt beauty and joy for ever.

When I touched her hand,
Currents raced tingling through me,
I kissed her,
All was oblivion but those lips,
Oh! she was so beautiful.

But alas! Alas my friends,
Time, that tireless teacher,
Time, the insatiable killer of joy,
And patient healer of all fevers,
Showed my bride was a woman.

Alas she is a woman,
A woman like my other wives,
Why can't she be my bride?
Why must she be like the others?
Must she join the harem?

Her eyes no longer speak love,
Only contempt when I rest.
Her words only harass me to work,
Her thoughts are problems,
Gone is my leisure, only worry remains.

Must I toil and sweat harder,
So our children can read?
Must I raise my voice in anger,
And sharpen my arrow and spears,

So my rich neighbours around
May not snatch her from me?

Must I forfeit my treasured leisure,
Must I spend sleepless nights,
Must my flying hours of youth
Be spent in cold calculating thought,
Must I age before my years,
So we can compare our home to others?

Oh that I could divorce you,
But God forbid! How I could, and say so!
Oh! Uhuru my love my sweet,
You are my bane, my life,
I love and hate you,
Your clutch is,

Uhuru my love, my Freedom.

JOHN MBITI

(Kenya)

The Moon

Thou in whom the rhythm of life is hid
Being born in the west
Maturing in eastern skies
Dying and buried
Beyond midnight in distant horizons
Yet rising from darkness and cold
Slowly from death and dissolution,
Bearing the numbers of fertility
The blessing of womankind.

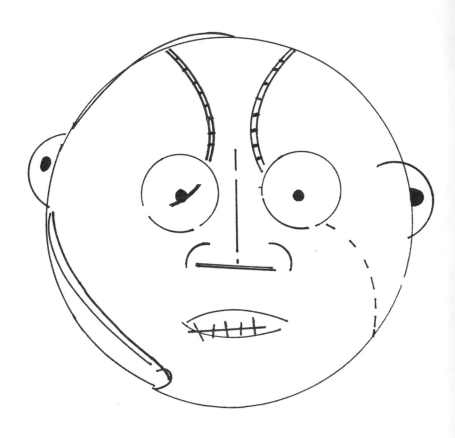

Thou giver of coolness and light
Spilling saliva of blessings to us on earth.
O animal great and round
The lonely neighbour
Whose tender light is earth's perpetual scent,
And thy rugged floor
The carpet of our spirit is.
For cycles upon cycles
Hast thou been
Free from human footprints and fingermarks,
But now art thou
Covered with dust of earth
Packed and sent in "Luna" and "Surveyor" forms.

Thou, our melting sister
Unkissed from birth by men,
We now encompass thee,
We now embrace,
We now trample upon thee,
We now shed our blood on thee,
At fantastic costs.
What mysteries of fertility and immortality,
These we now devise to know.

> For thou art chaste no more,
> Thou art one of us,
> Our flesh and our blood,
> The bride of earth.
> Oh burning fertility
> And mirror of immortality!
> We have loved thee from afar,
> But now we love thee in our arms.

JOHN ROBERTS

(Kenya)

The Searchers

We spend our lives walking in other people's towns,
Steps falling limp and echoless in the darkness,
Avoiding the pools which the street-lamps spill on the pavements
For fear of drowning our shadows as we wade.

The world is curtained behind its windows,
Watching us on its TV sets wondering:
Where are they going? Are their faces blank
Or is it the blade of the moon which scrapes them?

Our drums hang heavy on our shoulders
Which shouted their message so bravely by sunlight.

When the drumhead whispers back to the brush of a sleeve
We flinch and still it with our fingers.
I remember a dog ran out from an alley,
Sniffed my trousers, scented rags
And as I stooped to pat him ran back,
Claws clicking on the asphalt.

The moon, an eye blurred by cataract,
Studies a detail just behind us.

EDWIN WAIYAKI

(Kenya)

Despair

I have heard the leaves fall
From the trees with the soft patter
Of rats' feet on bare board.

The tiring mourners,
Lift gaunt hands skywards
In sad supplication.

They pray,
The stripped skeletons pray
To the season-god to return their summer.

And the god gives his answer
Of the hissing wind,
Chilling to the bone

Oh I have heard the leaves fall
From the trees like the soft tread
Of my beloved's sandals on bare boards.

And I,
Lone watcher in the woods
Lost in midst of evening twilight
Turn misted eyes to heaven
And I pray
To Him of autumn and of the howling wind:

I pray,
I stripped skeleton pray
Would she could wake—
Still, ashen figure in long robe of white;

I pray,
I stooped skeleton pray
Would she could rise,
Serene stricken figure in long robe of white.

But God gives his answer
In the scourging wind ...
Stinging to the bone.

FAARAH NUUR

(Somalia)

from *The Limits of Submission*

(This poem describes how the poet's clan had for long lived in submission to a stronger group, but were driven in the end to rebel and to assert their independence.)

Over and over again to people
I show abundant kindness.

.   .   .   .

If they are not satisfied
I spread out bedding for them
And invite them to sleep.

If they are still not satisfied,
The milk of the camel whose name is Suub
I milk three times for them,
And tell them to drink it up.

. . . .

If they are still not satisfied,
The homestead's ram,
And the fat he-goat I kill for them.

. . . .

If they are still not satisfied,
A beautiful girl
And her bridal house I offer them.

. . . .

If they are still not satisfied,
At the time of early morning prayers I prepare
The dark grey horse with black tendons,
And with the words "Praise to the Prophet" I take
The iron-shafted spear,
And drive it through their ribs
So that their lungs spew out;
Then they are satisfied!

Translators: B. W. Andrzejewski
I. M. Lewis

AHMAD NASSIR BIN JUMA BHALO

(Kenya)

A Male Lion, I Roar

1.

I roar again   O hunters, listen
I am looking for the gentlemen   with weapons on the shoulder
how is it that I haven't seen them yet?   what has prevented them?
you who are in hiding, come out   let us know the ripe from the
           raw.

2.

I speak to you, O men   who came to the hunt
and made me wild   so that I came out of the bush
why are you so far away now?   you do not come forward, why do
           you fear?
you who are in hiding, come out   let us know the ripe from the
           raw.

3.

Make good bullets   leave aside those bad ones
and arrows for piercing me   fill them up in the quiver
when you come let me eat up your flesh   after finishing the entrails
you who are in hiding, come out   let us know the ripe from the
           raw.

4.

Likewise the guides   whom you have in the hunt
who make themselves the best   at knowing the paths

while the lions grunt in the forest   what are their bullets waiting
                                                                        for?
you who are in hiding, come out   let us know the ripe from the
                                                                        raw.

5.

If you are archers   put your arrows to the bow
come and line up in front   let me see you on the boundary
whoever misses me, let me eat him up   I the lion, let me return to
                                                                the bush
you who are in hiding, come out   let us know the ripe from the
                                                                        raw.

.   .   .   .

7.

If it is a fight with spears   your hunting, my friends
I want one who is brave   for us to meet on the open spaces
the one whom I dodge does not survive   only his name will go
                                                                back home
you who are in hiding, come out   let us know the ripe from the
                                                                        raw.

.   .   .   .

9.

And if you are pit-trappers   well then, work hard, prepare the
                                                                    traps
snare me here where we can see things   put me in the cage
but if it fails   you will know who I am
you who are in hiding, come out   let us know the ripe from the
                                                                    raw.

10.

If you are noose-men   well then, work hard, fasten them
let the sides of the traps be of bamboo   cover the traps with leaves
let us see who is the doer   who I and you really are
you who are in hiding, come out   let us know the ripe from the
                                                                    raw.

.   .   .   .

12.

The end is in the twelfth verse   O orators, come then, orate
it is I the roaring lion   I who roar in the bush
whom these matters have annoyed   let him put his foot on the
                                                                    path
you who are in hiding, come out   let us know the ripe from the
                                                                    raw.

Translator: Lyndon Harries

The Eyes or the Heart?

1.

I bring accusations   let them reach every place
what has happened to me   let me explain it all
I, your friend, am grieved   I am not satisfied even when I eat
from thinking of the misfortune   that has happened to me.

2.

I blamed myself   I put the fault on my heart
for making me infatuated   while I loved the beloved
it came about that I had no time   even to want to sleep
because of the many anxieties   and the difficulty I found.

3.

So I took my heart to judge it   "Why give me this low state of
mind?"
and it answered, "Understand   I, your heart, am not at fault
you had better blame   what saw the beloved
they were the first to see   and to give me the desire."

4.

And when I went back to my eyes   to show them their fault
they also defended themselves   "It is the heart that brings un-
happiness
our job is just to look   we don't eat a thing
the heart loves the beloved   this is slander for us eyes."

5.

And my heart answered me   "Well then, say, what next!
this is useless, don't trouble yourself   looking for the one at fault
it is the eyes, it is because of them   that I like the place
because they are the ones who saw   and so I desired."

6.

On going back to my eyes   they would not accept responsibility
and they swore an oath to God   showing that they were not at
fault
and when I went back to my heart   it said, "Never, never in your
life
blame the one who saw   for it was then I began to desire."

7.

My friends, these things astonish me   these two things together
you will bring judgment   show me the one at fault
that I may know what to do   which one made me unhappy
either my eyes by seeing   or should I blame my heart?

8.

The end, I finish it   where it has stopped, O messenger
when He comes who is the Judge   to show me the one at fault
let him not make unlawful judgment   let him judge rightly
so that I may know the one with troubles   either the eyes or the
heart.

Translator: Lyndon Harries

JOSEPH GATUIRA

(Kenya)

Kariuki

The hour of midnight met with a gathering of mothers,
Their only talk—names upon names.
    "It will be my nephew" one said,
    "No, my sister's cousin." "Kirahiu
    Is the name or should it be Mwangi?"

Then I heard the delicate squeal of a baby
    (It is of an hour's age)
Caused no less than a whole village to awake.
    What causes them to awake?
    And an old man comes struggling into the house.

"How are you, Kariuki?" This he whispers
To the deaf stranger of this world.
    Whereupon the "Kariuki" begins its endless journey.
    It floats from mouth to mouth
    "It's a boy?" "Kariuki is born!"
    The old warrior is born again.

DAVID RUBADIRI

(Malawi)

from *Stanley Meets Mutesa*

. . . .

The thin weary line of carriers
With tattered dirty rags to cover their backs;

The battered bulky chests
That kept on falling off their shaven heads.
Their tempers high and hot
The sun fierce and scorching
With it rose their spirits
With its fall their hopes
As each day sweated their bodies dry and
Flies clung in clumps on their sweat-scented backs.
Such was the march
And the hot season just breaking.

Each day a weary pony dropped,
Left for the vultures on the plains;
Each afternoon a human skeleton collapsed,
Left for the Masai on the plains;
But the march trudged on
Its Khaki leader in front
He the spirit that inspired.

. . . .

The village looks on behind banana groves,
Children peer behind reed fences
Such was the welcome
No singing women to chaunt a welcome
Or drums to greet the white ambassador;
Only a few silent nods from aged faces

And one rumbling drum roll
To summon Mutesa's court to parley
For the country was not sure.

The gate of reeds is flung open,
There is silence
But only a moment's silence—
A silence of assessment.
The tall black king steps forward,
He towers over the thin bearded white man
Then grabbing his lean white hand
Manages to whisper
"Mtu Mweupe karibu"
White man you are welcome.
The gate of polished reed closes behind them
And the west is let in.

A Negro Labourer in Liverpool

I have passed him
Slouching on dark backstreet pavements
Head bowed—

Taut, haggard and worn.
A dark shadow amidst dark shadows.

I have lifted my face to his,
Our eyes met
But on his dark negro face
No sunny smile,
No hope or longing for a hope promised;
Only the quick cowed dart of eyes
Piercing through impassive crowds

Searching longingly for a face
Feeling painfully for a heart
That might flicker understanding.

This is him—
The negro labourer in Liverpool
That from his motherland,
A heart heavy
With the load of a century's oppression,
Gloriously sought for an identity
Grappled to clutch the fire of manhood
In the land of the free.
But here are only the free dead—
For they too are groping for a light.

Will that sun
That greeted him from his mother's womb
Ever shine again?
Not here—
Here his hope is the shovel,
And his fulfilment resignation.

OKOT P'BITEK

(Uganda)

from *Song of Lawino:*
An African Lament

Let No-One Uproot the
Pumpkin in the Old Homestead

(A Ugandan poem of more than two hundred pages that develops the African-European culture clash from the vantage point of a woman whose husband adopts Western ways)

· · · ·
Ocol says he is a modern man,
A progressive and civilized man,
He says he has read extensively and widely
And he can no longer live with a thing like me
Who cannot distinguish between good and bad,

He says I am just a village woman,
I am of the old type,
And no longer attractive.

· · · ·
Listen Ocol, my old friend,
The ways of your ancestors
Are good,
Their customs are solid
And not hollow
They are not thin, not easily breakable
They cannot be blown away
By the winds
Because their roots reach deep into the soil.

I do not understand
The ways of foreigners
But I do not despise their customs.
Why should you despise yours?

Listen, my husband,
You are the son of a Chief.
The pumpkin in the old homestead
Must not be uprooted!

.　.　.　.

Young girls
Whose breasts are just emerging
Smear *shea*-butter on their bodies,
The beautiful oil from Labwor-omor.

The aroma is wonderful
And their white teeth sparkle
As they sing
And dance fast
Among the dancers
Like small fish
In a shallow stream.

.　.　.　.

Who, but a witch
Would like to live
In a homestead
Where all the grown-ups
Are so clean after the rains
Because there are no
Muddy fat kids
To fall on their bosoms
After dancing in the rain
And playing in the mud!

At the lineage shrine
The prayers are for child birth!
At the *ogodo* dance

The woman who struts
And dances proudly,
That is the mother of many,

. . . .

Time has become
My husband's master
It is my husband's husband.
My husband runs from place to place
Like a small boy,
He rushes without dignity.

And when visitors have arrived
My husband's face darkens,
He never asks you in,
And for greeting
He says
"What can I do for you?"

. . . .

Children in our homestead
Do not sleep at fixed times.
When sleep comes
Into their head
They sleep.
When sleep leaves their head
They wake up.

When a child is dirty
Give him a wash,
You do not first look at the sun!

. . . .

You think of the pleasures
Of the girls
Dancing before their lovers,

Then you look at the teacher
Barking meaninglessly
Like the yellow monkey.

. . . .

O Lawino!
Chief of the girls
My love come
That I may elope with you
Daughter of the Bull
Come that I may touch you.

The teacher drummed
His meaningless phrases
Through his blocked nose;

. . . .

I know that this is not for nothing!

I know that someone is behind it.

. . . .

When your child is weak and listless,
When his energy fails him,
When he withdraws from the fight
For life, and gives up quickly,
It means his head has been captured,
And he is only a crawling corpse:

. . . .

Ten beautiful girls
Are walking in single file,
Along the pathway,
They carry axes
They are going to the bush
To split firewood,
In the grass lurks
The black mamba,
Its throat burning with venom.

The first three girls walk past,
Then the fourth and fifth,
And all nine girls go by,
And your daughter

Who is at the tail of the line
Is struck!

She stands there,
The reptile refuses to unhook its fangs,
She drinks a whole cup of death,
She gives a brief shriek
And mumbles some farewell
To her loving mother!
Then she drops
Dead!
She lies there
As if feigning death;
Her ripe breasts lift up their hands
And wail aloud,
Saying,

> *No mouths will suck us!*
> *Our tips will not be tickled!*
> *Our milk will rot in the earth!*

In battle
The hottest youths fight at the front,
Eager, angry, proud,
The youths think of their loves
And say,
It is the old ones
Who die in bed!
The spears of the foe
And their arrows
Rain like the hailstones,
Your son is struck
In the small of the back,
And the spear
Cuts through the liver
And the heart.

Other people's boys receive bruises
Others get cuts,
Many earn battle honours,
They return home
Blowing their horns, loud and clear!

And while others celebrate
And sing war songs,
You sing songs of praise,
Farewell songs to the dead!

Why should lightning
Seek out your husband
From his bed-room?
Other women's husbands
Are walking in the rain!

.   .   .   .

All misfortunes have a root,
The snake bite, the spear of the enemy,
Lightning and the blunt buffalo horn,
These are the bitter fruits
Grown on the tree of Fate.

.   .   .   .

There is no medicine in the hospital
For a mother's curse,
None for an uncle's curse!
And when your father's anger
Has boiled over
The white man's medicines
Are irrelevant and useless
Like the freak rains
In the middle of the dry season.

.   .   .   .

It is true
White man's medicines are strong,

But Acoli medicines
Are also strong.

The sick gets cured
Because his time has not yet come.
But when the day has dawned
For the journey to Pagak*
No one can stop you,
White man's medicines
Acoli medicines,
Crucifixes, rosaries,
Toes of edible rats,
The horn of the rhinoceros
None of them can block the path
That goes to Pagak!

When Death comes
To fetch you
She comes unannounced,
She comes suddenly
Like the vomit of dogs,
And when She comes
The wind keeps blowing
The birds go on singing
And the flowers
Do not hang their heads.
The *agoga* bird is silent
The *agoga* comes afterwards,
He sings to tell
That Death has been that way!

When Mother Death comes
She whispers
Come,

* The hereafter

And you stand up
And follow
You get up immediately,
And you start walking
Without brushing the dust
On your buttocks.

You may be behind
A new buffalo-hide shield,
And at the mock-fight,
Or in battle,
You may be matchless,

You may be hiding
In the hole
Of the smallest black insect,
Or in the darkest place
Where rats breast-feed their puppies,
Or behind the Agoro hills,

You may be the fastest runner,
A long distance runner,
But when Death comes
To fetch you
You do not resist,
You must not resist,
You cannot resist!

Mother Death
She says to her little ones,
Come!

Her little ones are good children,
Obedient,
Loyal,
And when Mother Death calls
Her little ones jump,

They jump gladly
For she calls
And offers simsim paste
Mixed with honey!
She says
My only child
Come,
Come, let us go.
Let us go!
And eat white-ants' paste
Mixed with *shea*-butter!
And who can resist that?

White diviner priests,
Acoli herbalists,
All medicine men and medicine women
Are good, are brilliant
When the day has not yet dawned

For the great journey
The last safari
To Pagak.

.   .   .

Listen, my clansmen,
I cry over my husband
Whose head is lost.
Ocol has lost his head
In the forest of books.

When my husband
Was still wooing me
His eyes were still alive,
His ears were still unblocked,

Ocol had not yet become a fool
My friend was a man then!

He had not yet become a woman,
He was still a free man,
His heart was still his chief.

My husband was still a Black man
The son of the Bull
The son of Agik
The woman from Okol
Was still a man,
An Acoli.

My husband has read much,
He has read extensively and deeply,
He has read among white men
And he is clever like white men

And the reading
Has killed my man,
In the ways of his people

. . . .

A good dog pleases its master,
It barks at night
And hunts in the salt lick
It chases away wild cats
That come to steal the chicken!
And when the master calls
It folds its tail between the legs.

The dogs of white men
Are well trained
And they understand English!

When the master is eating
They lie by the door
And keep guard
While waiting for left-overs.

But oh! Ocol
You are my master and husband,
You are the father of these children
You are a man,
You are you!

Do you not feel ashamed
Behaving like another man's dog
Before your own wife and children?

My husband, Ocol
You are a Prince
Of an ancient chiefdom,
Look,
There in the middle of the homestead
Stands your grandfather's Shrine,

Your grandfather was a Bull among men
And although he died long ago
His name still blows like a horn,
His name is still heard
Throughout the land.

. . . .

Has the Fire produced Ash?
Has the Bull died without a Head?
Aaa! A certain man
Has no millet field,
He lives on borrowed foods.

. . . .

O, my clansmen,
Let us all cry together!
Come,
Let us mourn the death of my husband,
The death of a Prince
The Ash that was produced

By a great Fire!
O, this homestead is utterly dead,
Close the gates
With *lacari* thorns,
For the Prince
The heir to the Stool is lost!
And all the young men
Have perished in the wilderness!

And the fame of this homestead
That once blazed like a wild fire
In a moonless night
Is now like the last breaths
Of a dying old man!

There is not one single true son left,
The entire village
Has fallen into the hands
Of war captives and slaves!
Perhaps one of our boys
Escaped with his life!
Perhaps he is hiding in the bush
Waiting for the sun to set!

But will he come?
Before the next mourning?
Will he arrive in time?

Bile burns my inside!
I feel like vomiting!

For all our young men
Were finished in the forest,
Their manhood was finished
In the class-rooms,

.   .   .   .

When you took the axe
And threatened to cut the *Okango*
That grows on the ancestral shrine
You were threatening
To cut yourself loose,
To be tossed by the winds
This way and that way
Like the dead dry leaves
Of the *olam* tree
In the dry season.

.   .   .   .

Let me dance before you,
My love,
Let me show you
The wealth in your house,
Ocol my husband,
Son of the Bull,
Let no one uproot the Pumpkin.

EPILOGUE

BUSHMAN

Song of the Rain

Under the sun
The earth is dry,
By the fire
Alone I cry.
All day long
The earth cries
For the rain to come.
All night my heart cries
For my hunter to come—
And take me away.

Oh! Listen to the wind,
You woman there;
The time is coming
The rain is near.
Listen to your heart,
Your hunter is here.
Translator: Laurens van der Post

NAR-GAD DIACK

(Senegal)

Day and night I scan the horizon
I have accompanied the sun to his final dwelling-place
Three evenings I have gazed at the glittering horizon
Where art thou my moon
May the hand of God protect thee
Thou art far away, my heart is clouded
My moon, I am thy star
Brighter I cannot shine
Thou art long in coming.

Translator: Lamine Diakhaté

ANNETTE M'BAYE

(Senegal)

Tomorrow belongs to God
But it also belongs to us.
Translator: Max Bilen

BIOGRAPHIES OF THE POETS

Biographies of the Poets

CHINUA ACHEBE

Novelist and short-story writer, he has also published criticism and lately some poetry. At present he is in the Institute of African Studies, University of Nigeria, Nsukka, and editor of *Okike,* a Nigerian literary journal.

CHRISTINA AMA ATA AIDOO

Christina Ama Ata Aidoo was born in Ghana and graduated from the University of Ghana, Legon, in 1963. Her short stories have appeared in *Black Orpheus,* and her verse in other journals and anthologies. She now does research and lectures in the Department of African Studies of the University of Ghana.

R. E. G. ARMATTOE

R. E. G. Armattoe was born in 1913 in Ghana. A medical doctor and anthropologist by profession, he practiced in Ireland for ten years. His poetry is published in two volumes, *Between the Forest and the Sea* and *Deep Down in the Blackman's Mind.* He was killed in an accident in Germany in 1953 while leading a delegation to the United Nations to canvass for the union of French and British Togo.

KOFI AWOONOR

Kofi Awoonor was born in 1935 at Keta in the Volta region of Ghana. Educated at Achimota College and the University of Ghana, he taught for some time at the university's Institute of African Studies, where he specialized in vernacular poetry. His poetry has appeared in numerous journals and he has published a volume of poetry, *Rediscovery,* and a novel. He is now teaching African literature at the State University of New York, Stony Brook.

KWESI BREW

Kwesi Brew was born in 1928 at Cape Coast in Ghana. Educated at the University of Ghana, he is now with the Ghanaian Foreign Service serving as Ghana's ambassador to Lebanon.

DENNIS BRUTUS

Dennis Brutus, a South African exile, was born in Rhodesia and educated in South Africa at the University of Fort Hare and Witwatersrand University. The author of several volumes of poetry, he has been active in campaigns for the release of South African political prisoners and the exclusion of apartheid teams from the Olympic games. He is presently teaching at Northwestern University, Evanston, Illinois.

Y. S. CHEMBA

Y. S. Chemba is the pen name of a senior civil servant in Uganda. Born in Budo near Kampala, he was educated at King's College, Budo; the Aga Khan School, Kampala; and University College, Nairobi.

J. P. CLARK

J. P. Clark—Nigerian poet, playwright, and journalist—was born in 1935 in the Ijaw country of the Niger delta. In addition to poems and essays in various journals, he has published three volumes of poetry and three plays, and has translated two volumes of traditional oral literature. He is now a lecturer in African literature at the University of Lagos, Nigeria.

BIRAGO DIOP

Birago Diop was born in 1906 in Dakar, Senegal. Educated in Senegal and France as a veterinary surgeon, he spent many years in Upper Volta as a veterinary officer. He is greatly interested in folklore and has published three volumes of folktales as well as *Leurres et luers,* a book of poetry.

DAVID DIOP

David Diop was born in 1927 in Bordeaux of Senegalese and Cameroonian descent. An invalid most of his short life, Diop was able to visit West Africa frequently. He was a regular contributor to *Présence Africaine* and published *Coups de Pilon,* a collection of poems. He died in 1960 in an air crash off Dakar.

MBELLA SONNE DIPOKO

Mbella Sonne Dipoko was born in Douala, Cameroon, in 1936. Educated in Cameroon and in Nigeria, he has worked for the Nigerian

Broadcasting Corporation in Lagos as a news reporter and on the staff of *Présence Africaine*. He is the author of two novels as well as stories and poetry published in various journals.

TSEGAYE GABRE-MEDHIN

Tsegaye Gabre-Medhin was born in 1935 in Ethiopia. Author of seventeen plays in Amharic as well as poetry published in various journals, he has served as acting director of the Haile Selassie Theatre in Addis Ababa.

JOSEPH GATUIRA

Born in Kenya, Joseph Gatuiria studied at Makerere College, Kampala, Uganda.

AIG HIGO

Aig Higo was born in Nigeria, and studied at the University of Ibadan in Nigeria and Leeds University in England. He has published poetry in the literary journal *Transition* and taught English at St. Andrew's College, Oyo, Nigeria.

AHMAD NASSIR BIN JUMA BHALO

Ahmad Nassir bin Juma Bhalo, born in 1937, works as a sign painter in Mombasa, Kenya. He studied in the Arab Boys' School there and attended a Moslem religious school in Mombasa. He has maintained a special interest in verse-composition for twelve years.

MAZISI KUNENE

Mazisi Kunene was born in 1930 in Durban, South Africa, where he studied at Natal University. He has lived in England since 1959, engaging in political work and studies of Zulu poetry and tradition. He has written a number of vernacular poems and plays, some of which have been published in South Africa.

CAMARA LAYE

Camara Laye was born in Kouroosa, Guinea, in 1924. He studied engineering in France and is the author of several novels, probably the best known being *L'Enfant Noir*. He is now living in Senegal.

ANNETTE M'BAYE

Annette M'Baye was born in 1927 in Sokhone, Senegal. She taught in Rufisque, Senegal, and in Paris. Since 1954 she has been involved with radio and journalism in Senegal and is currently with Radio Sénégal as well as being editor-in-chief of *Awa: Revue de la Femme Noire.*

JOHN MBITI

John Mbiti was born in 1931 in Kitui, Kenya. He was educated at Makerere College; Barrington College, where he was ordained; and Cambridge University. He has published several books in Kikamba, his mother tongue, and his poetry has appeared in various journals and anthologies as well as in *Poems of Nature and Faith.* He is now Professor of Religious Studies, Makerere University (formerly Makerere College).

FAARAH NUUR

Faarah Nuur died about 1930 in Somalia. A member of the Isaaq peoples, Faarah played an important part in emancipating his people from their bondage to the strong Iidegale clan, with which they had a long-standing association.

GABRIEL OKARA

Gabriel Okara was born in 1921 in Nigeria. Educated at Government College, Umuahia, he then became a bookbinder and began to write plays and features for broadcasting. His poetry has appeared regularly in *Black Orpheus,* and his novel *The Voice* was published in 1954. He is now with the Nigerian Ministry of Information in Port Harcourt.

UCHE OKEKE

Uche Okeke was born in 1933. He trained in art in Zaria, Nigeria, and in Munich. His work has been widely shown in Africa, Asia, Europe, and America. He lectures in painting and drawing in the Department of Fine Arts, University of Nigeria, Nsukka.

CHRISTOPHER OKIGBO

Christopher Okigbo was born in 1932 in Ojoto in Eastern Nigeria and died on the Nsukka battlefront in 1967 during the Nigerian Civil War. He studied classics at Ibadan University and taught at Fiditi Grammar School before joining the library staff at the University of Nigeria, Nsukka. He later became deeply involved in the Mbari Club, a pioneering literary society in Nigeria which published the journal *Black Orpheus*. His poetry has been published in three volumes.

DENNIS OSADEBAY

Chief Dennis Osadebay was born in 1911 in Asaba, Nigeria. He studied law in England and achieved success as a jurist, journalist, and politician, as well as a poet.

YAMBO OUOLOGUEM

Yambo Ouologuem was born in 1940 in Mali. He came to France in 1964, where he took French university degrees in literature, philosophy, and English. A publisher as well as writer, he produces school manuals for African students.

OKOT P'BITEK

Okot p'Bitek was born in 1931 at Bulu, northern Uganda. He has read education at Bristol, law at Aberystwyth, in Wales; and social anthropology at Oxford; has held posts at Makerere University and the Institute of African Studies of the University of Nairobi; and has been director of the National Cultural Course of Uganda.

L. D. RADITLADI

L. D. Raditladi belongs to the Bamangwato royal family of Botswana. He was educated at Fort Hare University College in South Africa.

JOHN ROBERTS

John Roberts is a former journalist on the *East African Standard* of Nairobi, and he worked with the African Service of the BBC in London. He is now managing editor of the *Africa Report* of New York and Washington.

DAVID RUBADIRI

David Rubadiri was born in 1930 in Malawi and educated at Makerere College and Cambridge University. A broadcaster while in England, he returned to Malawi to teach and has served in his country's Diplomatic Service.

Mabel Segun

Mabel Segun was educated at the C.M.S. Girls' School, Lagos, Nigeria, and the University of Ibadan. She has had a varied career as teacher, editor, broadcaster, and journalist. Her poetry has been published in *Black Orpheus* and in various anthologies, and her biographical book *My Father's Daughter* is used in Nigerian secondary schools.

Léopold Sédar Senghor

Léopold Sédar Senghor—poet, philosopher, and politician—was born at Joal, Senegal, in 1906. Educated at the Sorbonne, he has been at various times a deputy for Senegal in the French National Assembly, a minister in the French government, and since 1960 president of Senegal. One of the foremost advocates of Negritude, he has published six volumes of poetry.

Wole Soyinka

Wole Soyinka was born in 1934 at Abeokuta, Nigeria, and educated at the University of Ibadan and Leeds University. His plays have been performed widely in Africa, Europe, and America. He is also the author of a novel, *The Interpreters,* as well as several volumes of poetry. He is now with the School of Drama and Music, University of Ibadan.

Tchicaya U Tam'si

Tchicaya U Tam'si was born in 1931 at Mpili in the Middle Congo. In 1946 he accompanied his father, deputy from that colony, to France, where he studied at Orléans and Paris. He has contributed to many French reviews and written a number of African folklore programs for French radio. U Tam'si has published five volumes of poetry and is now with UNESCO's Department of Education in Paris.

B. W. Vilakazi

B. W. Vilakazi is known for his poetry and prose in Zulu published in South Africa. At the time of his death in 1947 he was on the staff of the Department of Bantu Languages at the University of Witwatersrand in Johannesburg.

EDWIN WAIYAKI

Born in Kikuyu, Kenya, in 1942, Edwin Waiyaki was educated at Besançon University and the Institut des Hautes Études d'Outre Mer in France. Currently with Oxford University Press in Nairobi, he will have a volume of his own poetry published soon by East African Publishing House.

OKOGBULE WONODI

Okogbule Wonodi was born in 1936 at Diobu near Port Harcourt, Nigeria. He studied at the University of Nigeria, Nsukka, and in the United States before assuming a position as lecturer at Nsukka. His poems and stories have been published in various journals and in his collections *Icheke* and *Dusts of Exile*. He is now working in Port Harcourt, Nigeria.

COPYRIGHT ACKNOWLEDGMENTS

Index of Titles

Africa, 115
Ancestral Faces, 12, 78
As Long as I Live, 139
Avenue: N.Y. City, The, 83

Baby Is a European, A, 42
Belly Remains, The (excerpt),
    120–121
Black Woman, 99–100
Bow Harp, 123
Breaths, 6

Chaka (excerpt), 102
Civil War Song, 46
Conflict, 80
Cradlesong (excerpt), 121

Death, 54
Defiance Against Force, 117
Despair, 149–150
Dirge, 56
Drum Chant, 44
Dry Season, The, 79

Efon (Buffalo), 43
Eyes or the Heart?, The,
    155–156

Farewell, 140
For He Was a Shrub Among the
    Poplars, 74
For Koras and Balafong
    (excerpt), 106–107

Girls' Secret Love Song, 26
Girl's Song, 28

Hail Him, 33

Home of Images, The, 96
Household Song, 25
Hunger, 36

I Shall Bring Honor to My Blood,
    120
"I Shall Quit," 32
Idandre (excerpts), 76–77
Immigrant, The, 91
In Blowing Your Nose, You Must
    Expose Your Teeth, 40
In Honor of a King Who
    Acquired Several Young
    Wives, 28
Inspection, 43
Invocation of the Creator, 21

Joal, 104

Kariuki, 8, 157
Keep It Dark!, 33

Lament, 49
Lament for the Dead Mother, 52
Lament of the Drums (excerpt),
    75
Lament of the Exiles, 90
Lazy Man, The, 39
Limits of Submission, The
    (excerpts), 150–151
Lonely Soul, The, 93
Long, Long You Have Held
    Between Your Hands, 109
Longing for Death, 52
Love Apart, 71
Love Songs, 24

Maiden's Song, 29

Male Lion, I Roar, A (excerpts),
  152–154
Marine Nocturne, 123
Mesh, The, 79
Modern Concert Song, 29
Moon, The (by John Mbiti),
  145, 147
Moon, The (Yoruba), 41
Moon Mist, 71
Motswasele's Farewell, 129–130
My Newest Bride, 143–145
Myself My Slogan, 89
My Wings Are Plucked, 37

Negro Labourer in Liverpool, A,
  159–160
New York, 110–112
Night Encounter, 87
Night Rain, 67–68
Night Song (excerpt), 70
Nightsong City, 134
Not Yet Enough, 39
Night of Sine, 100–101

Obolus (excerpt), 122
Oda Oak Oracle (excerpt), 94
One Night at Victoria Beach,
  63–64
Our History, 84–85
Ozidi Saga, A Lament from the, 53

Pain, 85
Pay Me a Visit, 37
Piano and Drums, 60
Pigeon-Hole, The, 80, 82
Poem (excerpt), 133
Poor Man, The, 35
Praise of a Child, 51
Prayer Before the Dead Body, 55
Prayer of Warriors, 48

Prayer to Masks, 105
Preoccupation, 34

Question, 95

Rama Kam, 5, 116
Rejoinder, 84
Renegade, The, 113
Requiem for a Black Girl
  (excerpt), 125

Sea, The, 136–138
Searchers, The, 148
Season, 77
Sebonwoma, 17
Shaka Zulu (excerpt), 135
Shango, I Prostrate to You Every
  Morning, 22
Skulls and Cups, 69
Sky, The, 41
Snow Flakes Sail Gently, The,
  62–63
Song (by J. P. Clark), 69
Song (Hima), 34
Song for an Absent Chief, 49
Song for the Sun that Dis-
  appeared Behind the Rain-
  clouds, 21–22
Song of Lawino: An African
  Lament (excerpts), 161–163,
  165–174
Song of Praise to the Creator
  (excerpt), 23
Song of the Rain, 177
Song of Young Men Working in
  the Gold Mines of Johannes-
  burg, 36
Song to the Envious, 45
Songs of Sorrow (excerpt), 92
Souffles, 117, 119
Spirit of the Wind, 59

Stanley Meets Mutesa (excerpts), 158–159
Streamside Exchange, 65
Sun, The, 40

To My Mother, 126
Train, The, 38
Trouble-Lover, The, 31

Umamina (excerpt), 130–132

Voices, 89

War Chant, 48
War Song, 46
Watermaid, 73
Worthless Lover, The, 27

Young Africa's Plea, 86

Zulu Lyric, A, 129

Index of Poets

Achebe, Chinua, 95
Aidoo, Christina Ama Ata, 17
Akan origin, 24, 33, 43, 49
Amhara origin, 25, 27
Armattoe, R. E. G., 93
Awoonor, Kofi, 92

Bhalo, Ahmad Nassir bin Juma, 152–156
Brew, Kwesi, 12, 78–79
Brutus, Dennis, 133–134
Bushman origin, 177

Chemba, Y. S., 143–145
Clark, J. P., 6, 7, 65, 67–70

Dahomean origin, 45, 56
Diack, Nar-gad, 177–178
Diaw, Ibra, 120
Dinka origin, 46
Diop, Birago, 5, 6, 117, 119
Diop, David, 5, 113, 115–117
Dipoko, Mbella Sonne, 84–85

Ekwere, John, 84
Ewe origin, 37, 40–41, 42, 52

Fon origin, 48

Gabre-Medhin, Tsegaye, 94
Ganda origin, 28
Gatuira, Joseph, 8, 157
Graft, Joe de, 10, 83

Haw origin, 53
Higo, Aig, 10, 89
Hima origin, 34

Hlubi origin, 28
Hottentot origin, 21, 46, 55

Iteso origin, 38

Kipsigi origin, 26
Kuba origin, 54
Kunene, Mazisi, 139–140

Laye, Camara, 126

Mabona, Mongameli, 136–138
M'Baye, Annette, 178
Mbiti, John, 145, 147
Mbundu origin, 34
Mulikita, F. M., 135

Nuur, Faarah, 150–151

Okara, Gabriel, 6, 59–60, 62–64
Okeke, Uche, 96
Okigbo, Christopher, 6, 71, 73–75
Osadebay, Dennis, 86
Ouologuem, Yambo, 125

p'Bitek, Okot, 10–11, 161–163, 165–174

Raditladi, L. D., 129–130
Roberts, John, 148
Rubadiri, David, 10, 158–160

Segun, Mabel, 9, 80, 82
Senghor, Léopold Sédar, 5, 8, 99–102, 104–107, 109–112
Sotho origin, 23
Soyinka, Wole, 6, 7, 13, 76–77
Swahili origin, 35

Thonga origin, 36
Tsaro-Wiwa, Ken, 8–9, 87, 89

U Tam'si, Tchicaya, 120–123

Vilakazi, B. W., 130–132
Vugusu origin, 48

Waiyaki, Edwin, 149–150

Wonodi, Okogbule, 9–10,
90–91

Yoruba origin, 21, 22, 31–32, 36–
37, 39–40, 43, 51

Zezuru origin, 33
Ziba origin, 29
Zulu origin, 3–4, 12, 29, 43, 129

Index of Translators

Adali-Mortty, Geormbeeyi, 37, 52
Akanji, Sangodare, 113
Allen, Samuel, 116–117, 119, 125
Andrzejewski, B. W., 150

Babalola, S. A., 31–32, 37, 39–40
Beier, Ulli, 21, 22, 36, 39, 41, 43,
    51, 54, 115
Bilen, Max, 178

Clark, J. P., 53
Cole, D. T., 129–130
Cruz, Clement da, 48

Diakhaté, Lamine, 120, 177–178
Doob, Leonard, 28, 29, 46

Ennis, Merlin, 34

Franz, G. H., 23

Gbadamosi, Bakare, 22, 36, 39,
    41, 43, 51

Harries, Lyndon, 35, 152–156
Herskovits, Frances, 45, 56
Hoh, Kafu, 40–41, 42

Jordan, A. C., 28
Junod, Henri A., 36

Kagwa, Apolo, 28
Kubik, Gerhard, 38

Lewis, I. M., 150–151
Lienhardt, Godfrey, 46

Maunick, Edouard J., 120–121
Mfeka, R. M., 130–132
Moore, Gerald, 121–123

Nketia, J. H. Kwabena, 24, 33,
    44, 49

Pankhurst, Sylvia, 25, 27
Peristiany, J. G., 26
Post, Laurens van der, 177

Rebse, Hermann, 29
Reed, John, 99–102, 104–107,
    109–112
Rutherfoord, Peggy, 129–132

Schultze, Leonhard, 46
Shapiro, Norman R., 126

Tracey, Hugh, 29, 33–34, 43, 129
Trilles, P., 22, 55

Wagner, Günter, 48
Wake, Clive, 99–102, 104–107,
    109–112, 117
Wiegrabe, P., 52

Index of First Lines

A baby is a European, 42
A child is like a rare bird, 51
Africa my Africa, 115
Ah, your sensual stare, 116
All was quiet in this park, 85
And the waves arrived, 84
Angled sunbeam lowered/like
    Jacob's ladder . . . , 95

"Be so good, my brother, 46
Black woman, African woman,
    O my mother, I think of you . . . ,
    126
Bright/with the armpit dazzle of
    a lioness, 73

Chaff is in my eye, 34
Chief they are bringing it, 44
Come here, my beloved, 29
Come, it is late in the day, 28
Come Mamina, 130
Coming up the stairs, 87

Day and night I scan the horizon,
    177
Don't preserve my customs, 86

Flying over Chicago that night
    he saw, 91
For he was a shrub among the
    poplars, 74
For me I shall buy an elderly one
    who will feed me, 28

Hail him, 33
He is patient, he is not angry, 21
Here we stand, 80

"How are you, Kariuki?" This he
    whispers, 8
How cold is an empty room, 49
How I wish I could pigeon-hole
    myself, 80
Hunger makes a person climb up
    to the ceiling, 36

I am sharpening my sword, 48
I bring accusations   let them
    reach every place, 155
I can look the sun in the face, 69
I have been singing, singing, 52
I have heard the leaves fall, 149
I have passed him, 159
I hear the cooing music of doves,
    90
I love you my child, 121
I met an old woman, 93
I refused, of course I did, 29
I roar again   O hunters, listen,
    152
I see it/There is no enjoying
    beyond death, 56
I shall bring honour to my blood,
    120
"I shall quit, 32
I shall return to the home of
    images, 96
I sleep long and soundly, 24
I would like to go, 17
In blowing your nose, you must
    expose your teeth, 40
Is this my country or is it mere
    soil, 129
It is not easy, Ukutee, 94

Joal!, 104

Keep it dark!, 33

Life,/like a gendarme's baton, 123
Listen more often to things than to
 beings, 177
Long, long you have held between
 your hands the black face of
 the warrior, 109
"Look, JP, 69

Masks! Masks!, 105
Mother dear, 52
My background is working class,
 89
My brother you flash your teeth
 in response to every hypocrisy,
 113
My mother lies a body before me,
 121
My wings are plucked;—woe's
 the day!, 37

Naked woman, dark woman, 99
New York! At first your beauty
 confused me, and your great
 long-legged golden girls, 110
Now, please sing the chorus of
 this song with me, 39
Now no more the paleface strangers, 84

O beloved farewell ... , 140
Ocean/Green or blue or iron-gray,
 136
Ocol says he is a modern man, 161
Of course the belly remains pure,
 120
Oh, Ozidi my man, my man, my
 man, 53

Ojo is his name, Ojo the Trouble-
 Lover, 31
Over and over again to people,
 150

Pay me a visit!, 37
Perfection ever rising to perfection, 23

River bird, river bird, 65
Rust is ripeness, rust, 77

Shaka was the Great Elephant,
 135
Shango, I prostrate to you every
 morning, 22
Shapes of men, 83
Sleep well, my love, sleep well,
 134
Somehow we survive, 133
Something has happened to me,
 92
Stones are very hard to break, 36

Take off your hat, 129
Tell me/what makes the sea grey,
 123
The Committee is at the school,
 43
The fire darkens, the wood turns
 black, 21
The gates of the underworld are
 closed, 55
The Giver of Life, 45
The hour of midnight met with a
 gathering of mothers, 157
The moon cannot fight, 41
The moon has ascended between
 us, 71
The night for me is filled with
 faces, 70

The night is coming. My lovely
Night the moon a golden coin,
102
The poor man knows not how to
eat with the rich man, 35
The sky at night is like a big city,
41
The snow flakes sail gently, 62
The sounds begin again, 12
The stars are departed, 71
The storks are coming now—, 59
The thin weary line of carriers,
158
The train /carries everybody/
everywhere, 38
The white man has brought his
war to the beach, 48
The wind comes rushing from the
sea, 63
The world was choked in wet
embrace, 76
The year is withering; the wind,
79
There is no needle without pierc-
ing point, 54
They came in hordes singing her
name, 143
They say/They will come and
take away/Our drumheads, 75
They sneaked into the limbo of
time, 78
They speak of taxes, 89
Thou in whom the rhythm of life
is hid, 145
Though the tribe holds a feast
against me, 46

To become a chief's favorite, 34
Toko'Waly my uncle, do you
remember those distant nights,
106
Tomorrow belongs to God, 178
Trousers of wind and buttons of
hail, 27

Under the sun, 177

We have come to the cross-roads,
79
We spend our lives walking in
other people's towns, 148
What have you done with my
letters, 125
What time of night it is, 67
When at break of day at a river-
side, 60
When I asked for him at Entoto,
he was towards Akaki, 25
When I still can remember, 139
When the cock crows, 39
When you hear thunder without
rain—, 43
Where are your children, sun?, 40
Woman, lay on my forehead
your perfumed hands, 100

You shake the waist—we shake,
26
You who bow you who mourn,
117
Your death has taken me by
surprise, 49

ABOUT THE COMPILER

Samuel Allen has been particularly interested in African poetry since his days as a student at the Sorbonne in Paris after World War II, when he met a number of African students and writers. Mr. Allen is himself a poet, and author of critical articles in the area of African and Afro-American literature. After graduation from Fisk University and Harvard Law School he began his career as a lawyer, but for years he has been writing poetry, much of it under the name of Paul Vesey. His poems are represented in many anthologies in this country and abroad, and his translation of Jean-Paul Sartre's *Black Orpheus* was published in London in 1960. Mr. Allen was Avalon Professor of Humanities at Tuskegee Institute from 1968 to 1970, and is now Professor of English at Boston University, where he is conducting a seminar in African literature.

ABOUT THE ARTIST

Like Samuel Allen, Romare Bearden studied at the Sorbonne after World War II, and he says that there he was affected by "the African concepts that run through the poetry of Senghor—the land, the beauty of a black woman, the protective presence of the dead, the acceptance of intuition. But the biggest thing I learned was reaching into the consciousness of black experience and relating it to universals."

Mr. Bearden was born in Charlotte, North Carolina, and educated at New York University. He studied drawing and painting at the Art Students League in New York City under George Grosz. His earliest exhibits were within the Harlem community during the late 1930's. Romare Bearden was honored with a retrospective exhibition at the Museum of Modern Art in New York City in 1971, and his works have been shown in leading museums and galleries throughout the world.